Fiona Mapp

Success

AQA
GCSE Mathematics
Higher
Workbook

Contents

Statistics and probability

Revised

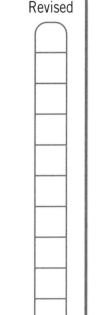

Number

Revised

Contents

Homework diary

TOPIC	SCORE
Collecting data	/17
Scatter graphs & correlation	/22
Averages 1	/30
Averages 2	/24
Cumulative frequency graphs	/25
Histograms	/14
Probability	/32
Fractions	/41
Approximations & checking calculations	/31
Percentages 1	/39
Percentages 2	/37
Fractions, decimals & percentages	/28
Recurring decimals & surds	/50
Ratio	/33
Indices	/48
Standard index form	/33
Upper & lower bounds of measurement	/31
Algebra & formulae	/40
Equations	/43
Equations & inequalities	/36
Advanced algebra & equations	/47
Direct & inverse proportion	/38
Linear graphs	/21
Non-linear graphs	/29
Advanced graphs	/24
Interpreting graphs	/17
Measures & measurement	/37
Transformations 1	/22
Transformations 2	/21
Bearings & scale drawings	/20
Loci & coordinates in 3D	/19
Angle properties of circles	/23
Pythagoras' theorem	/31
Trigonometry in right-angled triangles	/31
Application of trigonometry	/31
Further trigonometry	/37
Area of 2D shapes	/32
Volume of 3D shapes	/34
Further length, area & volume	/30
Similarity & congruency	/24
Vectors	/28

Homework diary

4

Revision & exam tips

Planning and revising:
- Mathematics should be revised **actively**. You should be doing **more than just reading**.
- Find out the dates of your first mathematics examination. Make an examination and revision timetable.
- After completing a topic in school, go through the topic again in the **GCSE AQA Success Revision Guide**. Copy out the **main points, results** and **formulae** into a notebook or use a **highlighter** to emphasise them.
- Try to write out the **key points** from **memory**. Check what you have written and see if there are any differences.
- Revise in short bursts of about **30 minutes,** followed by a **short break**.
- Learn **facts** from your exercise books, notebooks and the **Success Revision Guide**. **Memorise** any formulae you need to learn.
- Learn with a friend to make it easier and more fun!
- Do the **multiple-choice** and **short-answer** questions in this book and check your answers to see how much you know.
- Once you feel **confident** that you know the topic, do the **GCSE-style** questions in this book. **Highlight** the key words in the question, **plan** your answer and then go back and **check** that you have answered the question.
- **Make a note** of any topics that you do not understand and **go back through** the notes again.

Different types of questions:
- On the **GCSE Mathematics papers** you will have several types of questions:
  Calculate – In these questions you need to work out the answer. Remember that it is important to show full working out.
  Explain – These questions want you to explain, with a mathematical reason or calculation, what the answer is.
  Show – These questions usually require you to show, with mathematical justification, what the answer is.
  Write down or state – These questions require no explanation or working out.
  Prove – These questions want you to set out a concise logical argument, making the reasons clear.
  Deduce – These questions make use of an earlier answer to establish a result.

On the day:
- **Follow the instructions** on the exam paper. Make sure that you understand what any **symbols** mean.
- Make sure that you **read the question** carefully so that you give the answer that an examiner wants.
- Always **show your working;** you may pick up some marks even if your final answer is wrong.
- Do **rough calculations** to check your answers and make sure that they are **reasonable**.
- When carrying out a calculation, **do not round the answer until the end,** otherwise your final answer will not be as accurate as is needed.
- Lay out your working **carefully** and **concisely**. Write down the calculations that you are going to make. You usually get marks for showing a **correct method**.
- Make your drawings and graphs **neat** and **accurate**.
- Know what is on the **formula sheet** and make sure that you **learn** those formulae that are not on it.
- If you cannot do a question, **leave it out** and **go back** to it at the end.
- Keep an eye on the time. Allow enough time to check through your answers.
- If you finish early, check through everything very carefully and try to fill in any gaps.
- Try to write something even if you are not sure about it. Leaving an empty space will score you no marks.

Good luck!

Collecting data

Multiple-choice questions

Choose just one answer, a, b, c or d. Circle your choice.

1 What is the name given to data you collect yourself?

a) Continuous **b)** Primary **c)** Secondary **d)** Discrete

U1

(1 mark)

2 What is the name given to data that can take any value?

a) Continuous **b)** Primary **c)** Secondary **d)** Discrete

(1 mark)

3 A survey is being carried out on the number of hours some students spend watching television. In year 7 there are 240 students, year 8 has 300 students and year 9 has 460 students. John decides to use a stratified sample of 100 students. How many students should he ask from year 7?

a) 46 **b)** 30 **c)** 48 **d)** 24

(1 mark)

Score / 3

Short-answer questions

Answer all parts of each question.

1 Jim and Annabelle are designing a survey to use in their school. One of their questions is shown below.

U1

'How much time do you spend doing homework per night?'

0–1 hr	1–2 hr	2–3 hr	3–4 hr

What is the problem with this question? Rewrite the question to improve it.

....

....

....

(2 marks)

2 Laura conducts a survey of the students in her school. She decides to interview 100 students. Calculate the number of students she should choose from each year group to provide a representative sample. Complete the table below. 🖩

Year group	Number of students	Number of students in sample
7	120	
8	176	
9	160	
10	190	
11	154	

(3 marks)

Score / 5

Answer all parts of the questions. Show your workings (on a separate sheet of paper if necessary) and include the correct units in your answers.

1 A dentist wants to encourage her patients to have a balanced diet. The dentist has approximately 80 patients. She decides to do a survey about what type of diet her patients have.

(U1)

   a) The following is a question in the survey. Give a criticism of this survey question.
     'Do you have a healthy diet?'   Yes ☐   No ☐   Sometimes ☐   Every day ☐

                                                           (1 mark)

   b) The dentist decides to use one of two methods to do the survey.
     Method 1: Choose 50 patients at random.
     Method 2: Choose all the patients whose surnames begin with the letter 'A'.
     Which method will give the most reliable results? Give a reason for your choice.

                                                           (2 marks)

2 Robert is conducting a survey into the television habits of students at his school. One of the questions in his survey is: 'Do you watch a lot of television?'. His friend Jessica tells him that it is not a very good question. Write down two ways in which Robert could improve the question.

                                                           (2 marks)

3 The table shows the gender and number of students in each year group.

Year group	Number of boys	Number of girls	Total
7	160	120	280
8	108	132	240
9	158	117	275
10	85	70	155
11	140	110	250

Mark is carrying out a survey about how much pocket money students are given. He decides to take a stratified sample of 150 students from the whole school. Calculate how many in the stratified sample should be: 🖩

   a) students from year 8 _____   **b)** girls from year 11 _____   **(4 marks)**

Score   / 9

How well did you do?

(0–4) Try again   (5–9) Getting there   (10–13) Good work   (14–17) Excellent!

For more information on this topic, see pages 4–5 of your Success Revision Guide.

Scatter graphs & correlation

Multiple-choice questions

Choose just one answer, a, b, c or d. Circle your choice.

1 A scatter graph is drawn to show the height and weight of some students. What type of correlation is likely to be shown?

    a) Zero   **b)** Negative   **c)** Positive   **d)** Scattered

U1

(1 mark)

2 A scatter graph is drawn to show the maths scores and heights of a group of students. What type of correlation is likely to be shown?

    a) Zero   **b)** Negative   **c)** Positive   **d)** Scattered

(1 mark)

3 A scatter graph is drawn to show the age of some cars and their values. What type of correlation is likely to be shown?

    a) Zero   **b)** Negative   **c)** Positive   **d)** Scattered

(1 mark)

Score   / 3

Short-answer questions

Answer all parts of each question.

1 Some statements have been written on cards:

    (Positive correlation)   (Negative correlation)   (No correlation)

U1

Decide which card best describes the following relationships.

a) The outside temperature and the sales of ice lollies   (1 mark)

b) The outside temperature and the sales of woollen gloves   (1 mark)

c) The mass of a person and his/her waist measurement   (1 mark)

d) The height of a person and his/her IQ   (1 mark)

2 The scatter graph shows the marks scored in mathematics and physics examinations.

a) Describe the relationship between the mathematics and physics scores.

                                                (1 mark)

b) Draw a line of best fit on the scatter graph.   (1 mark)

c) Use your line of best fit to estimate the mathematics score that Jonathan is likely to obtain if he has a physics score of 75%.

                                                (1 mark)

Score   / 7

Answer all parts of the questions. Show your workings (on a separate sheet of paper if necessary) and include the correct units in your answers.

1 The table shows the ages of some children and the total number of hours of sleep they had between noon on Saturday and noon on Sunday.

(U1)

Age (years)	2	6	5	3	12	9	2	10	5	10	7	11	12	3
No. of hours of sleep	15	13.1	13.2	14.8	10.1	11.8	15.6	11.6	13.5	11.8	12.8	10.2	9.5	14

a) Plot the information from the table in the form of a scatter graph.   (4 marks)

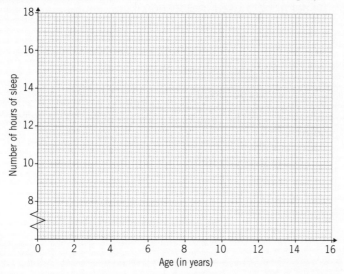

b) Describe the correlation between the age of the children and the total number of hours of sleep they had.

_____

_____   (2 marks)

c) Draw a line of best fit on your diagram.   (1 mark)

d) Estimate the total number of hours of sleep for a 4-year-old child.

_____   (2 marks)

e) Explain why the line of best fit only gives an estimate for the number of hours slept.

_____

_____   (2 marks)

f) A child psychologist states, '5-year-old children have between 15 and 16 hours of sleep a night.' Decide, based on the data above, whether the child psychologist is correct.

_____   (1 mark)

Score   / 12

How well did you do?

0–4 Try again   5–10 Getting there   11–15 Good work   16–22 Excellent!

For more information on this topic, see pages 8–9 of your Success Revision Guide.

Averages 1

Multiple-choice questions

Choose just one answer, a, b, c or d. Circle your choice.

1 What is the mean of this set of data? 2, 7, 1, 4, 2, 6, 2, 5, 2, 6

a) 4.2   **b)** 3.6   **c)** 3.7   **d)** 3.9

(U1)

(1 mark)

2 What is the median value of the set of data used in question 1?

a) 2   **b)** 3   **c)** 4   **d)** 5

(1 mark)

3 What is the range of this set of data? 2, 7, 1, 4, 11, 9, 6

a) 1   **b)** 6   **c)** 11   **d)** 10

(1 mark)

4 A dice is thrown and the scores are noted. The results are shown in the table below. What is the mean dice score? 🖩

Dice score	1	2	3	4	5	6
Frequency	12	15	10	8	14	13

a) 5   **b)** 3   **c)** 4   **d)** 3.5

(1 mark)

Score   / 4

Short-answer questions

Answer all parts of each question.

1 Here are some number cards: 8 7 11 4 2 1 3 12 4 4

(U1)

Decide whether the following statements are true or false.

a) The range of the number cards is 1–11 .... (1 mark)

b) The mean of the number cards is 5.6 .... (1 mark)

c) The median of the number cards is 5 .... (1 mark)

d) The mode of the number cards is 4 .... (1 mark)

2 A baked beans factory claims, 'On average, a tin of baked beans contains 141 beans.' In order to check the accuracy of this claim, a sample of 20 tins was taken and the number of beans in each tin counted.

Number of beans	137	138	139	140	141	142	143	144
Number of tins	1	1	1	2	5	4	4	2

a) Calculate the mean number of beans per tin. 🖩 .... (2 marks)

b) Explain briefly whether you think the manufacturer is justified in making its claim.

.... (1 mark)

3 The mean of 7, 9, 10, 18, x and 17 is 13. What is the value of x? .... (2 marks)

Score   / 9

Answer all parts of the questions. Show your workings (on a separate sheet of paper if necessary) and include the correct units in your answers.

1 Some students took a test. The table gives information about their marks in the test.

Mark	Frequency
3	2
4	5
5	11
6	2

U1

a) Write down the modal mark. .... (1 mark)

b) Work out the range of the marks. .... (1 mark)

c) Work out the mean mark. 🖩

....

.... (3 marks)

2 Simon sat three examinations. His mean score is 65. To pass the unit, he needs to get an average of 69. What score must he get in the fourth and final examination to pass the unit? 🖩

....

.... (3 marks)

3 A company employs 3 women and 7 men. The mean weekly wage of the 10 employees is £464. The mean weekly wage of the 3 women is £520. Calculate the mean weekly wage of the 7 men. 🖩

....

.... (4 marks)

4 10 boys and 10 girls are given 20 spellings to learn. Here is the number of correct answers for each girl:

14   15   13   14   10   12   8   18   19   11

The range of the boys' scores is 11.
The mean of the boys' scores is 14.

Use the data to investigate the hypothesis: 'Girls are better at spelling than boys.'

....

.... (5 marks)

Score   / 17

Statistics and probability

How well did you do?

0–10 Try again   11–17 Getting there   18–24 Good work   25–30 Excellent!

For more information on this topic, see pages 10–11 of your Success Revision Guide.

Averages 2

Multiple-choice questions

Choose just one answer, a, b, c or d. Circle your choice.

The following questions are based on the information given in the table opposite about the time taken in seconds to swim 50 metres.

Time (seconds)	Frequency (f)
$0 \leqslant t < 30$	1
$30 \leqslant t < 60$	2
$60 \leqslant t < 90$	4
$90 \leqslant t < 120$	6
$120 \leqslant t < 150$	7
$150 \leqslant t < 180$	2

(U1)

1 How many people swam 50 metres in less than 60 seconds?

a) 2   **b)** 4

c) 3   **d)** 6

(1 mark)

2 Which of the intervals is the modal class?

a) $60 \leqslant t < 90$ **b)** $120 \leqslant t < 150$ **c)** $30 \leqslant t < 60$ **d)** $90 \leqslant t < 120$

(1 mark)

3 Which of the class intervals contains the median value?

a) $90 \leqslant t < 120$ **b)** $150 \leqslant t < 180$ **c)** $120 \leqslant t < 150$ **d)** $60 \leqslant t < 90$

(1 mark)

4 What is the estimate for the mean time taken to swim 50 metres? 🖩

a) 105 seconds   **b)** 385 seconds   **c)** 100 seconds   **d)** 125 seconds

(1 mark)

Score   / 4

Short-answer questions

Answer all parts of each question.

Length (mm)	Number of seedlings
$0 \leqslant L < 10$	3
$10 \leqslant L < 20$	5
$20 \leqslant L < 30$	9
$30 \leqslant L < 40$	2
$40 \leqslant L < 50$	1

1 Information about the length of some seedlings is shown in the table opposite.

Calculate an estimate for the mean length of the seedlings. 🖩

Mean = ... mm

(U1)

(4 marks)

2 The stem-and-leaf diagram shows the marks gained by some students in a mathematics examination.

```
1 | 2 5 7
2 | 6 9
3 | 4 5 5 7
4 | 2 7 7 7 7
5 | 2
```

Key: 1 | 2 = 12 marks

Using the stem-and-leaf diagram, work out:

a) the mode ....

(1 mark)

b) the median ....

(1 mark)

c) the range. ....

(1 mark)

Score   / 7

GCSE-style questions

Answer all parts of the questions. Show your workings (on a separate sheet of paper if necessary) and include the correct units in your answers.

1 A psychologist records the times, to the nearest minute, taken by 20 students to complete a logic problem. Here are the results.

12	22	31	36	35	14	27	23	19	25
15	17	15	27	32	38	41	18	27	18

a) Draw an ordered stem-and-leaf diagram to show this information.

(3 marks)

b) What is the median time? _____ (1 mark)

2 Edward asks 100 people how much they spent last year on newspapers. The results are given in the table below.

Amount £ (x)	Frequency
$0 \leqslant x < 10$	12
$10 \leqslant x < 20$	20
$20 \leqslant x < 30$	15
$30 \leqslant x < 40$	18
$40 \leqslant x < 50$	14
$50 \leqslant x < 60$	18
$60 \leqslant x < 70$	3

a) Calculate an estimate of the mean amount spent on newspapers.

_____

(4 marks)

b) Explain briefly why this value of the mean is only an estimate.

_____

(1 mark)

c) Calculate the class interval in which the median lies.

_____

(2 marks)

d) Edward claims, 'The average amount of money spent on newspapers last year was between £10 and £20.' Explain whether you think that Edward's claim is correct.

_____

(2 marks)

Score   / 13

How well did you do?

| 0–6 | Try again | 7–11 | Getting there | 12–17 | Good work | 18–24 | Excellent! |

For more information on this topic, see pages 12–13 of your Success Revision Guide.

Cumulative frequency graphs

Multiple-choice questions

Choose just one answer, a, b, c or d. Circle your choice.

The data below shows the number of letters delivered to each of the 15 houses in Whelan Avenue (arranged in order of size). Use this information to answer the questions.

U1

0, 0, 1, 1, 1, 1, 1, 1, 2, 2, 2, 3, 4, 5, 5

1 What is the median number of letters delivered?

    a) 0   **b)** 2   **c)** 1   **d)** 5   (1 mark)

2 What is the lower quartile for the number of letters delivered?

    a) 0   **b)** 2   **c)** 3   **d)** 1   (1 mark)

3 What is the interquartile range for the number of letters delivered?

    a) 2   **b)** 3   **c)** 4   **d)** 5   (1 mark)

Score   / 3

Short-answer questions

Answer all parts of each question.

1 The table shows the marks of some year 10 pupils in their end-of-year maths exam.

U1

Examination mark	Frequency	Cumulative frequency
0–10	4	
11–20	6	
21–30	11	
31–40	24	
41–50	18	
51–60	7	
61–70	3	

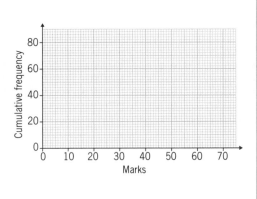

a) Complete the cumulative frequency column in the table above.   (2 marks)

b) Draw the cumulative frequency graph.   (3 marks)

c) From your graph, find the interquartile range. ....   (2 marks)

d) If 16 pupils were given a grade A in the examination, what is the minimum score needed for a grade A?

.... marks   (2 marks)

Score   / 9

Answer all parts of the questions. Show your workings (on a separate sheet of paper if necessary) and include the correct units in your answers.

1 The table shows the time, to the nearest minute, taken to run a marathon.

Time, t (minutes)	Frequency	Cumulative frequency
$120 < t \leqslant 140$	1	
$140 < t \leqslant 160$	8	
$160 < t \leqslant 180$	24	
$180 < t \leqslant 200$	29	
$200 < t \leqslant 220$	10	
$220 < t \leqslant 240$	5	
$240 < t \leqslant 260$	3	

a) Complete the table to show the cumulative frequency for this data.

(2 marks)

b) Draw the cumulative frequency graph for this data.

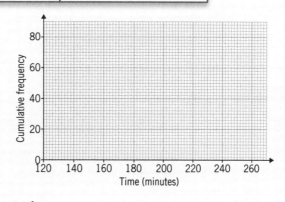

(3 marks)

c) Use your graph to work out an estimate for:

i) the interquartile range. _____ minutes

(2 marks)

ii) the number of runners with a time of more than 205 minutes. _____

(1 mark)

d) Draw a box plot for this data.

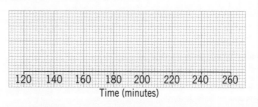

(3 marks)

e) The box plot shows the times, to the nearest minute, taken to run another marathon. Make two comparisons between the times taken to run the two marathons.

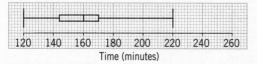

(2 marks)

Score   / 13

How well did you do?

| 0–6 | Try again | 7–12 | Getting there | 13–19 | Good work | 20–25 | Excellent! |

For more information on this topic, see pages 14–15 of your Success Revision Guide.

Histograms

Multiple-choice questions

Choose just one answer, a, b, c or d. Circle your choice.

The table shows the distance travelled to work by some employees. Use the information in the table to answer the questions below.

Distance, d (km)	Frequency
$0 \leqslant d < 5$	8
$5 \leqslant d < 15$	20
$15 \leqslant d < 20$	135
$20 \leqslant d < 30$	47
$30 \leqslant d < 50$	80

❶ Which class interval has a frequency density of 4.7?

a) $0 \leqslant d < 5$ b) $5 \leqslant d < 15$

c) $15 \leqslant d < 20$ d) $20 \leqslant d < 30$ (1 mark)

❷ The frequency density for one of the class intervals is 4. Which one is it?

a) $5 \leqslant d < 15$ b) $30 \leqslant d < 50$ c) $0 \leqslant d < 5$ d) $15 \leqslant d < 20$ (1 mark)

❸ Which class interval has the highest frequency density?

a) $0 \leqslant d < 5$ b) $15 \leqslant d < 20$ c) $20 \leqslant d < 30$ d) $5 \leqslant d < 15$ (1 mark)

❹ Which class interval has the lowest frequency density?

a) $0 \leqslant d < 5$ b) $5 \leqslant d < 15$ c) $15 \leqslant d < 20$ d) $30 \leqslant d < 50$ (1 mark)

U1

Score   / 4

Short-answer questions

Answer all parts of each question.

❶ The table and histogram give information about how long, in minutes, some students took to complete a maths problem.

Time, t (minutes)	Frequency
$0 < t \leqslant 5$	19
$5 < t \leqslant 15$	
$15 < t \leqslant 20$	16
$20 < t \leqslant 30$	
$30 < t \leqslant 45$	12

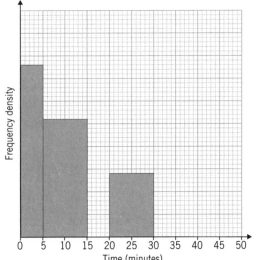

U1

a) Use the information in the histogram to complete the table.   (2 marks)

b) Use the table to complete the histogram.   (2 marks)

Score   / 4

Answer all parts of the questions. Show your workings (on a separate sheet of paper if necessary) and include the correct units in your answers.

1 The masses of some parcels are given in the table below.

Mass M (kg)	Frequency
$0 \leqslant M < 2$	14
$2 \leqslant M < 3$	8
$3 \leqslant M < 5$	13
$5 \leqslant M < 10$	14
$10 \leqslant M < 12$	7
$M \geqslant 12$	0

Draw a histogram to show the distribution of the mass of the parcels. Use a scale of 1cm to 2kg on the mass axis.

(3 marks)

2 Pierre recorded the length, in seconds, of some advertisements shown on television in a week. His results are shown in the histogram.

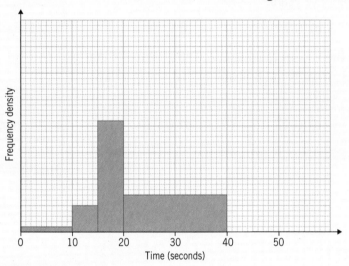

Use the information in the histogram to complete the table.

Time S (seconds)	Frequency
$0 \leqslant S < 10$	....
$10 \leqslant S < 15$	....
$15 \leqslant S < 20$	21
$20 \leqslant S < 40$	....
$S \geqslant 40$	0

(3 marks)

Score   / 6

How well did you do?

| 0–2 | Try again | 3–6 | Getting there | 7–10 | Good work | 11–14 | Excellent! |

For more information on this topic, see pages 16–17 of your Success Revision Guide.

Probability

Multiple-choice questions

Choose just one answer, a, b, c or d. Circle your choice.

1 The probability that Highbury football club win a football match is $\frac{12}{17}$. What is the probability that they do not win the football match?

    a) $\frac{5}{12}$ **b)** $\frac{17}{29}$ **c)** $\frac{12}{17}$ **d)** $\frac{5}{17}$ **(U1)**   (1 mark)

2 A fair dice is thrown 600 times. On how many of these throws would you expect to get a 4?

    a) 40   **b)** 600   **c)** 100   **d)** 580   (1 mark)

3 A fair dice is thrown 500 times. If a 6 comes up 87 times, what is the relative frequency?

    a) $\frac{1}{6}$ **b)** $\frac{87}{500}$ **c)** $\frac{10}{600}$ **d)** $\frac{1}{587}$ (1 mark)

4 The probability that it snows on Christmas Day is 0.2. What is the probability that it will snow on Christmas Day in two consecutive years?

    a) 0.04   **b)** 0.4   **c)** 0.2   **d)** 0.16   (1 mark)

5 The probability that Fiona is picked for the hockey team is 0.7. The probability that she is picked for the netball team is 0.3. What is the probability that she is picked for both teams?

    a) 1.0   **b)** 0.1   **c)** 0.12   **d)** 0.21   (1 mark)

Score   / 5

Short-answer questions

Answer all parts of each question.

Spinner 1

3	3
2	1

Spinner 2

6	2
3	1

1 Two spinners are spun at the same time and their scores are added.

Draw a sample space diagram or otherwise to find the probability of:

    a) a score of 4 _____   **b)** a score of 9 _____   **c)** a score of 1 _____   **(U1)**   (4 marks)

2 The probability that Michelle finishes first in a swimming race is 0.3
Michelle swims two races. Work out the probability that Michelle wins both races.

    (2 marks)

3 There are 13 counters in a bag: seven are red and the rest are white. A counter is picked at random, its colour noted and it is not replaced. A second counter is then chosen. What is the probability of choosing:

    a) two red counters? _____   (2 marks)

    b) a red and a white counter? _____   (3 marks)

Score   / 11

Answer all parts of the questions. Show your workings (on a separate sheet of paper if necessary) and include the correct units in your answers.

1 A bag contains different coloured beads. The probability of taking a bead of a particular colour at random is as follows:

Colour	Red	White	Blue	Pink
Probability	0.25	0.1		0.3

Jackie is going to take a bead at random and then put it back in the bag.

a) i) Work out the probability that Jackie will take out a blue bead. _____ (1 mark)

ii) Write down the probability that Jackie will take out a black bead. _____ (1 mark)

b) Jackie will take out a bead from the bag at random 200 times, replacing the bead each time. Work out an estimate for the number of times that Jackie takes a red bead.

_____ (2 marks)

2 Two fair dice are thrown together and their scores are added.

a) Work out the probability of a score of 7. _____ (2 marks)

b) Work out the probability of a score of 9. _____ (2 marks)

3 Kevin and Nathan challenge each other to a game of Monopoly and a game of pool. A draw is not possible in either game. The probability that Kevin wins at Monopoly is 0.4. The probability that Nathan wins at pool is 0.7.

a) Draw a probability tree diagram in the space below. 🖩

(3 marks)

b) What is the probability that Nathan wins both games? _____ (2 marks)

c) What is the probability that they win a game each? _____ (3 marks)

Score / 16

How well did you do?

| 0–11 | Try again | 12–21 | Getting there | 22–27 | Good work | 28–32 | Excellent! |

For more information on this topic, see pages 18–21 of your Success Revision Guide.

Fractions

Multiple-choice questions

Choose just one answer, a, b, c or d. Circle your choice.

1 In a class of 24 students, $\frac{3}{8}$ wear glasses. How many students wear glasses?

U1 U2 U3

   a) 9   **b)** 6   **c)** 3   **d)** 12

(1 mark)

2 Which one of these fractions is equivalent to $\frac{5}{9}$?

   a) $\frac{16}{27}$ **b)** $\frac{9}{18}$ **c)** $\frac{25}{45}$ **d)** $\frac{21}{36}$

(1 mark)

3 Work out the answer to $1\frac{5}{9} - \frac{1}{3}$

U2

   a) $\frac{1}{3}$ **b)** $1\frac{2}{9}$ **c)** $1\frac{4}{6}$ **d)** $\frac{4}{12}$

(1 mark)

4 Work out the answer to $\frac{2}{11} \times \frac{7}{9}$

   a) $\frac{14}{11}$ **b)** $\frac{14}{9}$ **c)** $\frac{14}{99}$ **d)** $\frac{2}{99}$

(1 mark)

5 Work out the answer to $\frac{3}{10} \div \frac{2}{3}$

   a) $\frac{9}{20}$ **b)** $\frac{6}{50}$ **c)** $\frac{6}{15}$ **d)** $\frac{4}{3}$

(1 mark)

Score   / 5

Short-answer questions

Answer all parts of each question.

1 Arrange these fractions in order of size, **smallest** first.

U2

   a) $\frac{2}{3}$ $\frac{4}{5}$ $\frac{1}{7}$ $\frac{3}{4}$ $\frac{1}{2}$ $\frac{3}{10}$

_____

(2 marks)

   b) $\frac{5}{8}$ $\frac{1}{3}$ $\frac{2}{7}$ $\frac{1}{9}$ $\frac{3}{4}$ $\frac{2}{5}$

_____

(2 marks)

2 Work out the answers to the following.

   a) $\frac{2}{9} + \frac{1}{3}$ _____   **b)** $\frac{7}{11} - \frac{1}{4}$ _____   **c)** $\frac{4}{7} \times \frac{3}{8}$ _____   **d)** $\frac{9}{12} \div \frac{1}{4}$ _____

   e) $2\frac{5}{7} - 1\frac{1}{21}$ _____   **f)** $\frac{4}{9} + \frac{3}{27}$ _____   **g)** $\frac{7}{12} \times 1\frac{1}{2}$ _____   **h)** $1\frac{4}{7} \div \frac{7}{12}$ _____

(8 marks)

3 State whether these statements are true or false.

   a) $\frac{4}{5}$ of 20 is bigger than $\frac{6}{7}$ of 14. _____

(1 mark)

   b) $\frac{2}{9}$ of 27 is smaller than $\frac{1}{3}$ of 15. _____

(1 mark)

4 In a class of 32 pupils, $\frac{1}{8}$ are left-handed. How many students are not left-handed?

_____

(1 mark)

Score   / 15

Answer all parts of the questions. Show your workings (on a separate sheet of paper if necessary) and include the correct units in your answers.

1 Work out the following. (U2)

   a) $\frac{2}{3} + \frac{4}{5}$ _____ (1 mark)

   b) $3\frac{9}{11} - 2\frac{1}{3}$ _____ (1 mark)

   c) $\frac{2}{7} \times \frac{4}{9}$ _____ (1 mark)

   d) $\frac{3}{10} \div \frac{2}{5}$ _____ (1 mark)

2 A flag has three colours: red, white and blue. $\frac{1}{3}$ of the flag is red; $\frac{2}{5}$ of the flag is white. What fraction of the flag is blue?

_____

_____ (3 marks)

3 Charlotte's take-home pay is £930. She gives her mother $\frac{1}{3}$ of this and spends $\frac{1}{5}$ of the £930 on going out. What fraction of the £930 is left? How much is this?

_____

_____ (3 marks)

4 Reece works 15 hours per week. He earns £6 per hour. Reece saves $\frac{1}{5}$ of his earnings each week. He needs to save £120 for a holiday. How many weeks does it take Reece to save £120?

_____

_____ weeks (4 marks)

5 Gill says, 'Since 5 is halfway between 4 and 6, then $\frac{1}{5}$ will be halfway between $\frac{1}{4}$ and $\frac{1}{6}$.' Gill is wrong. Show that $\frac{1}{5}$ is not halfway between $\frac{1}{4}$ and $\frac{1}{6}$.

_____

_____ (3 marks)

6 Sam is 60 years old. His son Thomas is $\frac{2}{3}$ of Sam's age. His grand-daughter Amy is $\frac{3}{10}$ of Sam's age. How many years older than Amy is Thomas?

_____

_____ years (4 marks)

Score   / 21

Number

How well did you do?

| 0–14 | Try again | 15–22 | Getting there | 23–32 | Good work | 33–41 | Excellent! |

For more information on this topic, see pages 28–29 of your Success Revision Guide.

21

Approximations & checking calculations

Multiple-choice questions

Choose just one answer, a, b, c or d. Circle your choice.

1 A carton of orange juice costs 79p. Estimate the cost of 402 cartons of orange juice.

    a) £350   **b)** £250   **c)** £400   **d)** £320

U1 U2 (1 mark)

2 A school trip is organised. 396 pupils are going on the trip. Each coach seats 50 pupils. Approximately how many coaches are needed?

    a) 12   **b)** 5   **c)** 8   **d)** 10

(1 mark)

3 Estimate the answer to the calculation $\frac{(4.2)^2}{107}$

    a) 16   **b)** 1.6   **c)** 0.16   **d)** 160

(1 mark)

4 Estimate the answer to the calculation 27×41

    a) 1107   **b)** 1200   **c)** 820   **d)** 1300

(1 mark)

5 Round 5379 to 3 significant figures.

    a) 538   **b)** 5370   **c)** 537   **d)** 5380

U1 U2 U3 (1 mark)

Score / 5

Short-answer questions

Answer all parts of each question.

1 Round each of the numbers in the following calculations to 1 significant figure then work out an approximate answer.

U1 U2

    a) $\frac{(32.9)^2}{9.1}$ (1 mark)

    b) $\frac{(906 \div 31.4)^2}{7.1 + 2.9}$ (1 mark)

2 State whether each statement is true or false.

U1 U2 U3

    a) 2.742 rounded to 3 significant figures is 2.74 (1 mark)

    b) 2793 rounded to 2 significant figures is 27 (1 mark)

    c) 32 046 rounded to 1 significant figure is 40 000 (1 mark)

    d) 14.637 rounded to 3 significant figures is 14.6 (1 mark)

3 Work out the following on your calculator.
Give your answers to 3 significant figures.

U1 U3

    a) $\frac{4.2 \times (3.6 + 5.1)}{2 - 1.9}$ **b)** $6 \times \sqrt{\frac{12.1}{4.2}}$

    c) $\frac{12^5}{4.3 \times 9.15}$ **d)** $\frac{4\cos 30° + 2\sin 60°}{4^3}$

(4 marks)

Score / 10

Answer all parts of the questions. Show your workings (on a separate sheet of paper if necessary) and include the correct units in your answers.

1 The highest mountains on each continent are shown in the table below.   U1 U2 U3

Mountain peak	Continent	Height (m)
Mount Everest	Asia	8850
Aconcagua	South America	6959
Mount McKinley	North America	6194
Kilimanjaro	Africa	5895
Mount Elbrus	Europe	5642
Vinson Massif	Antarctica	4897
Carstensz Pyramid	Oceania	4884

a) Which two mountains would have the same height if their heights were rounded to 2 significant figures?

_____   (1 mark)

b) Gareth says, 'The difference in height between Mount Everest and Carstensz Pyramid is about 4000m'. Is Gareth correct? Give a reason for your answer.

_____   (2 marks)

2 a) Use your calculator to work out the value of the following. Write down all the figures on your calculator display. 🖩   U1 U3

$\dfrac{27.1 \times 6.2}{38.2 - 9.9}$ _____   (2 marks)

b) Round each of the numbers in the above calculation to 1 significant figure and obtain an approximate answer.

_____   (3 marks)

3 a) Use your calculator to work out the value of the following. Write down all the figures on your calculator display. 🖩

$\dfrac{(12.6 + 9.41)^2}{2.7 - 1.06}$ _____   (2 marks)

b) Round your answer to 3 significant figures. _____   (1 mark)

4 Use your calculator to work out the value of the following. 🖩

$\dfrac{\sqrt{(4.9^2 + 6.3)}}{2.1 \times 0.37}$ _____   (2 marks)

5 Estimate the answer to the following.   U2

$\dfrac{4.9 \times (6.1^2 + 2.8^2)}{10.02 \times 5}$ _____   (3 marks)

Score   / 16

Number

How well did you do?

(0–11) Try again   (12–19) Getting there   (20–26) Good work   (27–31) Excellent!

For more information on this topic, see pages 32–33 of your Success Revision Guide.

Percentages 1

Number

Multiple-choice questions

Choose just one answer, a, b, c or d. Circle your choice.

1 A CD player costs £60 in a sale after a reduction of 20%. What was the original price of the CD player? 📟

   a) £48   **b)** £70   **c)** £72   **d)** £75

(U1)

(1 mark)

2 Work out 17.5% of £60.

   a) £9   **b)** £15   **c)** £10.50   **d)** £12.50

(U1)(U2)

(1 mark)

3 Work out 10% of £850.

   a) £8.50   **b)** £0.85   **c)** £85   **d)** £42.50

(1 mark)

4 In a survey, 17 people out of 25 said they preferred type A cola. What percentage of people preferred type A cola?

   a) 68%   **b)** 60%   **c)** 72%   **d)** 75%

(U1)(U2)(U3)

(1 mark)

5 A new car was bought for £15 000. Two years later it was sold for £12 000. What was the percentage loss?

   a) 25%   **b)** 20%   **c)** 80%   **d)** 70%

(U2)

(1 mark)

Score   / 5

Short-answer questions

Answer all parts of each question.

1 The cost of a ticket for a pop concert has risen by 15% to £23. What was the original price of the ticket? 📟

£ ....

(U1)

(2 marks)

2 The price of a CD player has been reduced by 20% in a sale. It now costs £180. What was the original price? 📟

£ ....

(2 marks)

3 Work out the answers to the following.

   a) 20% of £60 ....   **b)** 30% of £150 ....

   c) 5% of £80 ....   **d)** 12.5% of 40g ....

(U1)(U2)

(4 marks)

4 Last year, Colin earned £25 500. This year he has a 3% pay rise. How much does Colin now earn? 📟

£ ....

(U1)(U3)

(2 marks)

5 A coat costs £140. In a sale it is reduced to £85. What is the percentage reduction? 📟

.... %

(2 marks)

Short-answer questions (cont.)

6 Lucinda scored 58 out of 75 in a test. What percentage did she get, correct to 1 d.p.?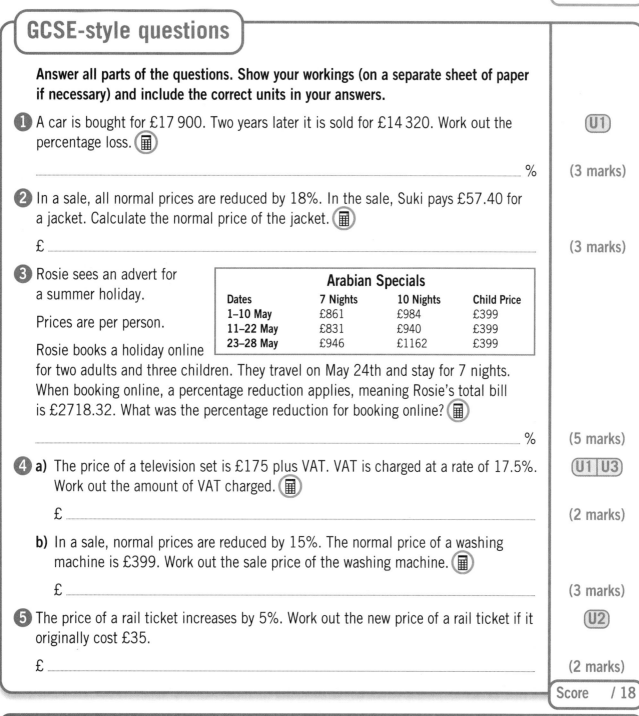

U1 U3

.... %   (2 marks)

7 12 out of 30 people wear glasses. What percentage wear glasses?

.... %   (2 marks)

Score   / 16

GCSE-style questions

Answer all parts of the questions. Show your workings (on a separate sheet of paper if necessary) and include the correct units in your answers.

1 A car is bought for £17 900. Two years later it is sold for £14 320. Work out the percentage loss.

U1

.... %   (3 marks)

2 In a sale, all normal prices are reduced by 18%. In the sale, Suki pays £57.40 for a jacket. Calculate the normal price of the jacket.

£ ....   (3 marks)

3 Rosie sees an advert for a summer holiday.

Prices are per person.

Arabian Specials			
Dates	7 Nights	10 Nights	Child Price
1–10 May	£861	£984	£399
11–22 May	£831	£940	£399
23–28 May	£946	£1162	£399

Rosie books a holiday online for two adults and three children. They travel on May 24th and stay for 7 nights. When booking online, a percentage reduction applies, meaning Rosie's total bill is £2718.32. What was the percentage reduction for booking online?

.... %   (5 marks)

4 a) The price of a television set is £175 plus VAT. VAT is charged at a rate of 17.5%. Work out the amount of VAT charged.

U1 U3

£ ....   (2 marks)

b) In a sale, normal prices are reduced by 15%. The normal price of a washing machine is £399. Work out the sale price of the washing machine.

£ ....   (3 marks)

5 The price of a rail ticket increases by 5%. Work out the new price of a rail ticket if it originally cost £35.

U2

£ ....   (2 marks)

Score   / 18

How well did you do?

| 0–11 | Try again | 12–20 | Getting there | 21–30 | Good work | 31–39 | Excellent! |

Number

For more information on this topic, see pages 34–35 of your Success Revision Guide.

Percentages 2

Number

Multiple-choice questions

Choose just one answer, a, b, c or d. Circle your choice.

1 £2000 is invested in a savings account. Compound interest is paid at 2.1% p.a. How much interest is paid after two years? 🔲

    a) £4   **b)** £5.20   **c)** £2.44   **d)** £84.88

(U1)

(1 mark)

2 A bike was bought for £120. Each year it depreciated in value by 10%. What was the bike worth two years later?

    a) £97.20   **b)** £98   **c)** £216   **d)** £110

(1 mark)

3 Roberto has £5000 in his savings account. Simple interest is paid at 3% p.a. How much does he have in his savings account at the end of the year?

    a) £4850   **b)** £5010   **c)** £5150   **d)** £5140.50

(U2)

(1 mark)

4 Lily earns £23 500. National Insurance (NI) is deducted at 11%. How much NI must she pay?

    a) £2250   **b)** £2585   **c)** £2605   **d)** £21 385

(1 mark)

Score   / 4

Short-answer questions

Answer all parts of each question.

1 Scarlett has £6200 in her savings account. If compound interest is paid at 2.7% p.a., how much interest will she have earned in total after three years? 🔲

  £ ....

(U1)

(2 marks)

2 A motorbike is bought for £9000. Each year it depreciates in value by 12%. Work out the value of the motorbike after two years. 🔲

  £ ....

(2 marks)

3 A house was bought for £112 000. After the first year the price had increased by 8%; during the second year it increased by a further 12%. What is the house now worth? 🔲

  £ ....

(2 marks)

4 Petrol cost 113.7 pence per litre. The price increased by 2%. Six months later it increased again, by 5%. How much does a litre of petrol now cost? 🔲

  ....p

(2 marks)

5 A meal costs £143. VAT at 17.5% is added. What is the final price of the meal?

  £ ....

(U1 U2)

(2 marks)

6 VAT of 5% is added to a gas bill of £72. Find the total amount to be paid.

  £ ....

(2 marks)

Score   / 12

Answer all parts of the questions. Show your workings (on a separate sheet of paper if necessary) and include the correct units in your answers.

1 £7000 is invested for three years at 6% compound interest. Work out the total interest earned over the three years. 🔲   (U1)

£ ....   (3 marks)

2 Nigel opened an account with £450 at his local bank. After one year, the bank paid him interest. He then had £465.75 in his account.

a) Work out, as a percentage, his bank's interest rate. 🔲

....   (3 marks)

b) Sarah opened an account at the same bank as Nigel. She invested £700 for two years at 4% compound interest. How much money did she have in her account after two years?

£ ....   (3 marks)

3 William invests £2000 in each of his two bank accounts. The terms of the bank accounts are shown below.

Super Savers	Nest Egg
Simple interest at 4% per annum	Compound interest at 4% per annum

Work out the difference between the two bank accounts in the amount of interest that William receives at the end of two years. 🔲

£ ....   (4 marks)

4 A vintage bottle of champagne was valued at £42 000 on 1 January this year. The value of the champagne is predicted to increase at a rate of R% per annum. The predicted value, £V, of the champagne after n years is given by the formula
$V = 42\,000 \times (1.045)^n$

a) Write down the value of R. ....   (1 mark)

b) Find the predicted value of the champagne after eight years. 🔲

£ ....   (2 marks)

5 Sara bought a car for £14 000. Each year the value of the car depreciated by 10%. Work out the value of the car two years after she bought it.

£ ....   (3 marks)

6 In a sale, a shop took 20% off normal prices. On 'Terrific Tuesday', it took a further 20% off its sale prices. Bibi says, 'That means there was 40% off the normal prices.' Bibi is wrong. Explain why.   (U2)

....   (2 marks)

Score   / 21

Number

How well did you do?

| 0–8 | Try again | 9–15 | Getting there | 16–27 | Good work | 28–37 | Excellent! |

For more information on this topic, see pages 36–37 of your Success Revision Guide.

Fractions, decimals & percentages

Multiple-choice questions

Choose just one answer, a, b, c or d. Circle your choice.

1 What is $\frac{3}{5}$ as a percentage?

   a) 30%   **b)** 25%   **c)** 60%   **d)** 75%

U1 U2 U3

(1 mark)

2 What is $\frac{2}{3}$ written as a decimal?

   a) 0.77   **b)** 0.$\dot{6}$ **c)** 0.665   **d)** 0.6

(1 mark)

3 What is the smallest value in this list of numbers? 29%, 0.4, $\frac{3}{4}$, $\frac{1}{8}$

   a) 29%   **b)** 0.4   **c)** $\frac{3}{4}$ **d)** $\frac{1}{8}$

(1 mark)

4 What is the largest value in this list of numbers? $\frac{4}{5}$, 80%, $\frac{2}{3}$, 0.9

   a) $\frac{4}{5}$ **b)** 80%   **c)** $\frac{2}{3}$ **d)** 0.9

(1 mark)

5 What is $\frac{5}{8}$ as a decimal?

   a) 0.625   **b)** 0.425   **c)** 0.125   **d)** 0.725

(1 mark)

Score   / 5

Short-answer questions

Answer all parts of each question.

1 Decide whether the following calculations give the same answer for this instruction: increase £40 by 20%.

U1 U2

Jack says: 'Multiply 40 by 1.2'   Hannah says: 'Work out 10%, double it and then add 40'

Explain your reasoning.

_____

_____

(2 marks)

2 The table shows equivalent fractions, decimals and percentages. Fill in the gaps.

U1 U2 U3

Fraction	Decimal	Percentage
$\frac{2}{5}$		
		5%
	0.$\dot{3}$	
	0.04	
		25%
$\frac{1}{8}$		

(6 marks)

Score   / 8

Number

28

GCSE-style questions

Answer all parts of the questions. Show your workings (on a separate sheet of paper if necessary) and include the correct units in your answers.

1 Philippa is buying a new television. She sees three different advertisements for the same television set.

Ed's Electricals

TV normal price

£250

Sale 10% off

Sheila's Bargains

TV £185 plus

VAT at $17\frac{1}{2}$%

GITA's TV SHOP

Normal price

£290

Sale: $\frac{1}{5}$ off normal price

a) Philippa wants to buy her television from one of these shops, as cheaply as possible. Which shop should she choose and how much cheaper is it than the most expensive shop? 🖩

_____

(5 marks)

b) The price of the television in a fourth shop is £235. This includes VAT at 17.5%. Work out the cost of the television before VAT was added. 🖩

£ _____

(3 marks)

2 A sundial is being sold in two different garden centres. The cost of the sundial is £89.99 in both garden centres. Both garden centres have a promotion.

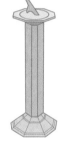

Gardens Are Us ⟨ Sundial 22% off ⟩

Rosebushes ⟨ Sundial $\frac{1}{4}$ off ⟩

In which garden centre is the sundial cheaper? Explain your answer.

_____

_____

(2 marks)

3 Write this list of seven numbers in order of size. Start with the smallest number.

25% $\frac{1}{3}$ 0.27 $\frac{2}{5}$ 0.571   72% $\frac{1}{8}$

_____

(3 marks)

4 Place these fractions in order of size, smallest first.

$\frac{2}{3}, \frac{1}{10}, \frac{5}{8}, \frac{3}{5}, \frac{9}{10}$

(2 marks)

Score   / 15

U1 **(3 marks)** etc.

U1

U1 | U2 | U3

U2

Number

How well did you do?

| 0–6 | Try again | 7–13 | Getting there | 14–22 | Good work | 23–28 | Excellent! |

For more information on this topic, see page 38 of your Success Revision Guide.

Recurring decimals & surds

Multiple-choice questions

Choose just one answer, a, b, c or d. Circle your choice.

U2

1 Which fraction is the same as $0.\dot{5}$?

   a) $\frac{1}{2}$ **b)** $\frac{5}{10}$ **c)** $\frac{5}{9}$ **d)** $\frac{5}{8}$ (1 mark)

2 Which fraction is equivalent to $0.\dot{6}\dot{3}...$?

   a) $\frac{63}{100}$ **b)** $\frac{6}{99}$ **c)** $\frac{636}{999}$ **d)** $\frac{7}{11}$ (1 mark)

3 Which fraction is equivalent to $0.2\dot{1}...$?

   a) $\frac{19}{90}$ **b)** $\frac{21}{99}$ **c)** $\frac{211}{999}$ **d)** $\frac{2}{9}$ (1 mark)

4 Which expression is equivalent to $\sqrt{12}$?

   a) $2\sqrt{6}$ **b)** $2\sqrt{3}$ **c)** $6\sqrt{2}$ **d)** $3\sqrt{2}$ (1 mark)

5 Which expression is equivalent to $\frac{1}{\sqrt{3}}$?

   a) $\frac{\sqrt{3}}{3}$ **b)** $\frac{\sqrt{3}}{9}$ **c)** $\frac{9}{\sqrt{3}}$ **d)** $\frac{3}{\sqrt{3}}$ (1 mark)

Score   / 5

Short-answer questions

Answer all parts of each question.

1 Match each of the recurring decimals to the equivalent fraction.

U2

      $0.\dot{3}$ $\frac{7}{9}$

      $0.\dot{7}$ $\frac{244}{333}$

      $0.\dot{2}\dot{4}$ $\frac{13}{30}$

      $0.\dot{7}3\dot{2}$ $\frac{1}{3}$

      $0.4\dot{3}$ $\frac{8}{33}$ (5 marks)

2 Find the fraction that is equivalent to $0.1\dot{2}\dot{5}$. Express the fraction in its simplest form.

      (2 marks)

3 Express each of the following in the form $a\sqrt{b}$, where a and b are integers and b is as small as possible.

   a) $\sqrt{24}$ (1 mark)

   b) $\sqrt{75}$ (1 mark)

   c) $\sqrt{48} + \sqrt{12}$ (2 marks)

   d) $\sqrt{80} + \sqrt{20}$ (2 marks)

4 Rationalise the denominator $\frac{3}{\sqrt{2}}$

      (2 marks)

Score   / 15

Answer all parts of the questions. Show your workings (on a separate sheet of paper if necessary) and include the correct units in your answers.

1 a) Change the decimal $0.\overset{\cdot\cdot}{54}$ into a fraction in its simplest form.

(U2)

(2 marks)

   b) Write the recurring decimal $0.0\overset{\cdot\cdot}{26}$ as a fraction.

(2 marks)

2 a) Find the value of $\sqrt{3} \times \sqrt{27}$

(1 mark)

   b) $\sqrt{3} + \sqrt{27} = a\sqrt{3}$, where a is an integer. Find the value of a.

(1 mark)

   c) Find the value of $\dfrac{\sqrt{3} + \sqrt{12}}{\sqrt{75}}$

(3 marks)

3 a) Show that $\sqrt{60} = 2\sqrt{15}$

(1 mark)

   b) Expand and simplify $(\sqrt{3} + \sqrt{10})^2$

(2 marks)

   c) Rationalise the denominator $\dfrac{1}{\sqrt{3}}$

(2 marks)

4 Write down the recurring decimal $0.1\overset{\cdot\cdot}{23}$ in the form $\frac{a}{b}$ where a and b are integers.

(2 marks)

5 Simplify $(4 - \sqrt{3})^2$

(2 marks)

6 Express $\dfrac{\sqrt{125} + \sqrt{50}}{\sqrt{5}}$ in the form $a + \sqrt{b}$

(4 marks)

7 Work out $\dfrac{(2 - \sqrt{2})(4 + 3\sqrt{2})}{2}$

Give your answer in the form $a + b\sqrt{c}$

(3 marks)

8 Write down the recurring decimal $0.\overset{\cdot\cdot}{75}$ as a fraction in its simplest form.

(2 marks)

9 Prove that the recurring decimal $0.\overset{\cdot\cdot}{45}$ is $\frac{5}{11}$

(3 marks)

Score   / 30

Number

How well did you do?

| 0–14 | Try again | 15–28 | Getting there | 29–41 | Good work | 42–50 | Excellent! |

For more information on this topic, see page 39 of your Success Revision Guide.

Ratio

Multiple-choice questions

Choose just one answer, a, b, c or d. Circle your choice.

1 What is the ratio 6 : 18 written in its simplest form?

    a) 3 : 1   **b)** 3 : 9   **c)** 1 : 3   **d)** 9 : 3

U1 U2 U3

(1 mark)

2 Write the ratio 200 : 500 in the form $1 : n$

    a) 1 : 50   **b)** 1 : 5   **c)** 1 : 25   **d)** 1 : 2.5

(1 mark)

3 A recipe for 4 people needs 800g of flour. How much flour is needed for 6 people?

    a) 12g   **b)** 120g   **c)** 12kg   **d)** 1200g

(1 mark)

4 If 9 oranges cost £1.08, how much would 14 similar oranges cost?

    a) £1.50   **b)** £1.68   **c)** £1.20   **d)** £1.84

(1 mark)

5 If £140 is divided in the ratio 3 : 4, what is the size of the larger share?

    a) £45   **b)** £60   **c)** £80   **d)** £90

U2

(1 mark)

Score   / 5

Short-answer questions

Answer all parts of each question.

1 Write down the ratio 10 : 15 in the form $1 : n$

U1 U2 U3

(1 mark)

2 7 bottles of lemonade have a total capacity of 1680ml. Work out the total capacity of 5 similar bottles. 🔢

_____ ml (1 mark)

3 It takes 6 people 3 days to dig and lay a cable. How long would it take 4 people?

_____ days (2 marks)

4 If £1 = 1.09 euros (€), change €726 into pounds. Give your answer correct to the nearest penny. 🔢

£ _____ (2 marks)

5 **a)** Increase £4.10 in the ratio 2 : 5 _____

U2

(1 mark)

    b) Decrease 120g in the ratio 5 : 2 _____

(1 mark)

6 Mrs London inherited £55 000. She divided the money between her children in the ratio 3 : 3 : 5. How much did the child with the largest share receive?

£ _____ (2 marks)

Score   / 10

Answer all parts of the questions. Show your workings (on a separate sheet of paper if necessary) and include the correct units in your answers.

1 13 metres of fabric costs £107.12. Work out the cost of 25 metres of the same fabric.

£ ....

U1 | U2 | U3

(2 marks)

2 James uses these ingredients to make 12 buns:

| 50g butter |
| 40g sugar |
| 2 eggs |
| 45g flour |
| 15ml milk |

James wants to make 18 similar buns.
Write down how much of each ingredient
he needs for 18 buns.

Butter .... g   Sugar .... g

Eggs ....   Flour .... g

Milk .... ml

(3 marks)

3 It takes 3 builders 16 days to build a wall. All the builders work at the same rate. How long would it take 8 builders to build a wall of the same size?

.... days

(3 marks)

4 The table below shows the minimum ratio of staff to children in a crèche.

Age	Minimum adult : child ratio
Children under 2 years	1 : 3
Children aged 2 years	1 : 4
Children aged 3–5 years	1 : 8

On a Tuesday, the crèche has 17 children under 2 years, 14 children aged 2 years and 26 children aged 3–5 years. If the children of each age group are in separate rooms, how many staff must the manager have working on a Tuesday? 🖩

....

(3 marks)

5 Vicky and Tracy share £14 400 in the ratio 4 : 5. How much does each of them receive?

Vicky: £ ....   Tracy: £ ....

U2

(3 marks)

6 Peas are sold in two different-sized tins. A small tin holds 142g and costs 24p. A large tin holds 300g and costs 49p. Which tin is the better buy? You must show full working out to justify your answer. 🖩

....

U3

(4 marks)

Score   / 18

Number

How well did you do?

0–11 **Try again**   12–19 **Getting there**   20–26 **Good work**   27–33 **Excellent!**

For more information on this topic, see pages 40–41 of your Success Revision Guide.

Indices

Multiple-choice questions

Choose just one answer, a, b, c or d. Circle your choice.

1 In index form, what is the value of $8^3 \times 8^{11}$?

(U2)

    a) 8^{14} **b)** 8^{33} **c)** 64^{14} **d)** 64^{33} (1 mark)

2 In index form, what is the value of $(4^2)^3$?

    a) 12^2 **b)** 4^5 **c)** 4^6 **d)** 16^6 (1 mark)

3 What is the value of 5^0?

    a) 5   **b)** 0   **c)** 25   **d)** 1   (1 mark)

4 What is the value of 5^{-2}?

    a) $\frac{1}{25}$ **b)** -5   **c)** 25   **d)** -25   (1 mark)

5 In index form, what is the value of $7^{-12} \div 7^2$?

    a) 7^{10} **b)** 7^{-14} **c)** 7^{14} **d)** 7^{-10} (1 mark)

Score   / 5

Short-answer questions

Answer all parts of each question.

1 Decide whether each of these expressions is true or false.

(U2)

    a) $a^4 \times a^5 = a^{20}$ (1 mark)

    b) $2a^4 \times 3a^2 = 5a^8$ (1 mark)

    c) $10a^6 \div 2a^4 = 5a^2$ (1 mark)

    d) $20a^4b^2 \div 10a^5b = 20a^{-1}b$ (1 mark)

    e) $(2a^3)^3 = 6a^9$ (1 mark)

    f) $4^0 = 1$ (1 mark)

2 Simplify the following expressions.

    a) $(5a)^0 =$ **b)** $(2a^2)^4 =$

    c) $12a^4 \div 16a^7 =$ **d)** $(3a^2b^3)^3 =$ (4 marks)

3 Write these using negative indices.

    a) $\frac{4}{x^2} =$ **b)** $\frac{a^2}{b^3} =$ **c)** $\frac{3}{y^5} =$ (3 marks)

4 Evaluate these expressions.

    a) $25^{-\frac{1}{2}}$ **b)** $49^{\frac{3}{2}}$ **c)** $\left(\frac{4}{5}\right)^2$ **d)** $81^{-\frac{3}{4}}$ (4 marks)

Score   / 17

Answer all parts of the questions. Show your workings (on a separate sheet of paper if necessary) and include the correct units in your answers.

1 Olivia says $m^3 \times m^2 = m^6$. Olivia is wrong. Explain why Olivia is wrong.   (U2)

_____

_____

(2 marks)

2 Simplify the following:

a) $p^3 \times p^4$ .... (1 mark)

b) $\dfrac{n^3}{n^7}$ .... (1 mark)

c) $\dfrac{a^3 \times a^4}{a}$ .... (1 mark)

d) $\dfrac{12a^2b}{3a}$ .... (1 mark)

3 Evaluate the following:

a) 3^0 ....   **b)** 9^{-2} ....   **c)** $3^4 \times 2^3$ ....   **d)** $64^{\frac{2}{3}}$ ....

e) $125^{-\frac{1}{3}}$ ....   (5 marks)

4 a) Evaluate the following:

i) 8^0 .... (1 mark)

ii) 4^{-2} .... (1 mark)

iii) $\left(\frac{4}{9}\right)^{-\frac{1}{2}}$ .... (1 mark)

b) Write the following as a single power of 5.

$\dfrac{5^7 \times 5^3}{(5^2)^3}$ .... (2 marks)

5 Evaluate the following, giving your answers as fractions.

a) 5^{-3} .... (1 mark)

b) $\left(\frac{2}{3}\right)^{-2}$ .... (1 mark)

c) $(8)^{-\frac{2}{3}}$ .... (1 mark)

6 Simplify the following, leaving your answer in the form 2^n.

a) $4^{-\frac{1}{2}}$ .... (1 mark)

b) $\dfrac{2^7 \times 2^9}{2^{-4}}$ .... (1 mark)

c) $(\sqrt{2})^5$ .... (1 mark)

7 Simplify the following expressions.

a) $(5x)^3$ ....   **b)** $(y^5)^4$ ....   **c)** $(3y)^{-3}$ ....   **d)** $(2xy^3)^5$ ....   (4 marks)

Score   / 26

Number

How well did you do?

| 0–12 | Try again | 13–23 | Getting there | 24–37 | Good work | 38–48 | Excellent! |

For more information on this topic, see pages 42–43 of your Success Revision Guide.

Standard index form

Multiple-choice questions

Choose just one answer, a, b, c or d. Circle your choice.

1 What is this number written in standard form? 42 710

U1 U2

    a) 42.71×10^3 **b)** 4.271×10^4 **c)** 4271.0×10 **d)** 427.1×10^2 (1 mark)

2 What is 6.4×10^{-3} written as an ordinary number?

    a) 6400   **b)** 0.0064   **c)** 64   **d)** 0.064   (1 mark)

3 What is 2.7×10^4 written as an ordinary number?

    a) 27 000   **b)** 0.27   **c)** 270   **d)** 0.000 27   (1 mark)

4 What is $(4 \times 10^9) \times (2 \times 10^6)$ worked out and written in standard form?

U2

    a) 8×10^{54} **b)** 8×10^{15} **c)** 8×10^3 **d)** 6×10^{15} (1 mark)

5 What is $(3 \times 10^4)^2$ worked out and written in standard form?

    a) 9×10^6 **b)** 9×10^8 **c)** 9×10^9 **d)** 3×10^8 (1 mark)

Score   / 5

Short-answer questions

Answer all parts of each question.

1 State whether each of the statements is true or false.

U1 U2

    a) 4710 is 4.71×10^3 written in standard form.   (1 mark)

    b) 249 000 is 24.9×10^4 written in standard form.   (1 mark)

    c) 0.047 is 47×10^{-3} written in standard form.   (1 mark)

    d) 0.000 009 6 is 9.6×10^{-7} written in standard form.   (1 mark)

2 Work out the following calculations. Give your answer in standard form.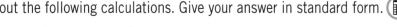

U1

    a) $(2.1 \times 10^7) \times (3.9 \times 10^{-4})$ (1 mark)

    b) $(6.3 \times 10^{-4}) \times (1.2 \times 10^6)$ (1 mark)

    c) $(1.2 \times 10^{-9}) \div (2 \times 10^{-3})$ (1 mark)

3 The mass of an atom is 2×10^{-23} grams. What is the total mass of 9×10^{15} of these atoms? Give your answer in standard form.

        (3 marks)

4 Work out the following calculations. Give your answer in standard form.

U2

    a) $(4 \times 10^6) \times (2 \times 10^9)$ (1 mark)

    b) $(7 \times 10^{-3}) \times (2 \times 10^6)$ (1 mark)

    c) $(9 \times 10^{12}) \div (3 \times 10^{-4})$ (1 mark)

Score   / 13

Answer all parts of the questions. Show your workings (on a separate sheet of paper if necessary) and include the correct units in your answers.

1 If $a = 3.2 \times 10^4$ and $b = 2 \times 10^{-3}$, calculate the answer to $\dfrac{b^2}{a+b}$ giving your answer in standard form, correct to 3 significant figures.

U1

(2 marks)

2 3.8×10^8 seeds weigh 1 kilogram.

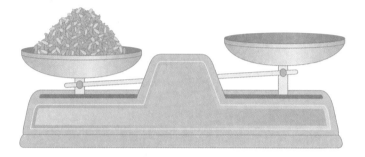

Each seed weighs the same. Calculate the weight in grams of one seed.
Give your answer in standard form, correct to 2 significant figures. 🖩

.... g   (2 marks)

3 The mass of Saturn is 5.7×10^{26} tonnes. The mass of the Earth is 6.1×10^{21} tonnes. How many times heavier is Saturn than the Earth? Give your answer in standard form, correct to 1 decimal place. 🖩

(3 marks)

4 a) Five investors buy a warehouse for £4.3 million. They each contribute the same amount. How much does each investor pay? Give your answer in standard form. 🖩

£ ....   (2 marks)

b) After converting the warehouse into luxury apartments, the investors make a profit of £3.1 million. How much profit does each investor make? Give your answer in standard form. 🖩

£ ....   (2 marks)

5 a) i) Write the number 2.07×10^5 as an ordinary number.

U2

(1 mark)

ii) Write the number 0.000 046 in standard form.

(1 mark)

b) Multiply 7×10^4 by 5×10^7
Give your answer in standard form.

(2 marks)

Score   / 15

Number

How well did you do?

| 0–9 Try again | 10–19 Getting there | 20–27 Good work | 28–33 Excellent! |

For more information on this topic, see pages 44–45 of your Success Revision Guide.

37

Upper & lower bounds of measurement

Multiple-choice questions

Choose just one answer, a, b, c or d. Circle your choice.

1 The length of an object is 5.6cm, correct to the nearest millimetre. What is the lower bound of the length of the object?

   a) 5.56cm   **b)** 5.55cm   **c)** 5.64cm   **d)** 5.65cm

(U1)

(1 mark)

2 The mass of an object is 2.23 grams, correct to 2 decimal places. What is the upper bound of the mass of the object?

   a) 2.225g   **b)** 2.234g   **c)** 2.235g   **d)** 2.32g

(1 mark)

3 A hall can hold 40 people to the nearest 10. What is the upper bound for the number of people in the hall?

   a) 45   **b)** 35   **c)** 44   **d)** 36

(1 mark)

4 A square has a length of 3cm to the nearest centimetre. What is the lower bound for the perimeter of the square?

   a) 12cm   **b)** 10cm   **c)** 10.4cm   **d)** 14cm

(1 mark)

5 Using the information given in the previous question, what is the upper bound for the area of the square?

   a) 6.25cm^2 **b)** 9cm^2 **c)** 12.5cm^2 **d)** 12.25cm^2

(1 mark)

Score   / 5

Short-answer questions

Answer all parts of each question.

1 A book has a mass of 112 grams, correct to the nearest gram.

Write down the lowest possible mass of the book. _____ g

(U1)

(1 mark)

2 $a = \dfrac{(3.4)^2 \times 12.68}{2.4}$

3.4 and 2.4 are correct to 1 decimal place. 12.68 is correct to 2 decimal places. Which of the following calculations gives the lower bound for a and the upper bound for a? (Write down the letters.)

   a) $\dfrac{(3.45)^2 \times 12.685}{2.35}$ **b)** $\dfrac{(3.35)^2 \times 12.675}{2.35}$ **c)** $\dfrac{(3.45)^2 \times 12.685}{2.45}$

   d) $\dfrac{(3.45)^2 \times 12.675}{2.35}$ **e)** $\dfrac{(3.35)^2 \times 12.675}{2.45}$

Lower bound _____ Upper bound _____

(2 marks)

3 To the nearest centimetre, $a = 3$cm, $b = 5$cm. Calculate the lower bound for ab. 🖩

_____ cm^2

(2 marks)

Score   / 5

GCSE-style questions

Answer all parts of the questions. Show your workings (on a separate sheet of paper if necessary) and include the correct units in your answers.

1 $p = 3.1$cm and $q = 4.7$cm, correct to 1 decimal place.　　　　　　　(U1)

　a) Calculate the upper bound for the value of $p + q$ 🖩

　..

　..　　(2 marks)

　b) Calculate the lower bound for the value of $\frac{p}{q}$
　　Give your answer correct to 3 significant figures.

　..

　..　　(3 marks)

2 A ball is thrown vertically upwards with a speed V metres per second.
　The height, H metres, to which it rises is given by:

　$H = \dfrac{V^2}{2g}$ where g m/s^2 is the acceleration due to gravity.

　$V = 32.6$ correct to 3 significant figures. $g = 9.8$ correct to 2 significant figures.

　Calculate the difference between the lower and upper bound of H.
　Give your answer correct to 3 significant figures. 🖩

　... m　　(5 marks)

3 Jaydn drove for 146 miles, correct to the nearest mile. He used 15.6 litres of petrol
　to the nearest tenth of a litre.

　Petrol consumption $= \dfrac{\text{Number of miles travelled}}{\text{Number of litres of petrol used}}$

　Jaydn makes the claim that his petrol consumption is less than 9.3 miles per litre.
　Explain whether Jaydn's claim is correct. You must show full working out to justify
　your answer. 🖩

　..　　(3 marks)

4 The volume of a cube is given as 62.7cm^3, correct to 1 decimal place. Find the upper
　and lower bounds for the length of an edge of this cube. 🖩

　Lower bound = ...　　Upper bound = ...　　(4 marks)

5 The mass of an object is measured as 120g and its volume as 630cm^3.
　Both of these measurements are correct to 2 significant figures. Find the range
　of possible values for the density of the object. 🖩

　..　　(4 marks)

　　　　　　　　　　　　　　　　　　　　　　　　　　　　　Score　　/ 21

Number

How well did you do?

| 0–6 | Try again | 7–12 | Getting there | 13–21 | Good work | 22–31 | Excellent! |

For more information on this topic, see pages 46–47 of your Success Revision Guide.

Algebra & formulae

Multiple-choice questions

Choose just one answer, a, b, c or d. Circle your choice.

1 $P = a^2 + b$. Rearrange this formula to make a the subject.

(U2)

a) $a = \pm\sqrt{(P - b)}$ b) $a = \pm\sqrt{(P + b)}$ c) $a = \frac{P - b}{2}$ d) $a = \frac{P + b}{2}$

(1 mark)

2 What is the expression $7a - 4b + 6a - 3b$ when it is fully simplified?

(U2) (U3)

a) $7b - a$ b) $13a + 7b$ c) $a - 7b$ d) $13a - 7b$

(1 mark)

3 If $m = \sqrt{\frac{r^2 p}{4}}$ and $r = 3$ and $p = 6$, what is the value of m to 1 decimal place? 🖩

a) 13.5   b) 182.3   c) 3.7   d) 3

(1 mark)

4 What is $(n - 3)^2$ when it is multiplied out and simplified?

a) $n^2 + 9$ b) $n^2 + 6n - 9$ c) $n^2 - 6n - 9$ d) $n^2 - 6n + 9$

(1 mark)

5 Factorising $n^2 + 7n - 8$ gives which of the following?

a) $(n - 2)(n - 6)$ b) $(n - 2)(n + 4)$ c) $(n - 1)(n + 8)$ d) $(n + 1)(n - 8)$

(1 mark)

Score   / 5

Short-answer questions

Answer all parts of each question.

1 Rearrange each of the formulae below to make b the subject.

(U2)

a) $p = 3b - 4$ .... (1 mark)

b) $y = \frac{b^2 - 6}{4}$ .... (1 mark)

c) $5(n + b) = 2b + 2$ .... (1 mark)

2 John buys b books costing £6 each and p magazines costing 67 pence each.
Write down a formula for the total cost (T) of the books and magazines.

(U2) (U3)

$T =$ .... (2 marks)

3 $a = \frac{b^2 + 2c}{4}$ 🖩

a) Calculate a if $b = 2$ and $c = 6$ .... (1 mark)

b) Calculate a if $b = 3$ and $c = 5.5$ .... (1 mark)

c) Calculate b if $a = 25$ and $c = 18$ .... (1 mark)

4 Factorise the following expressions.

a) $10n + 15$ ....   b) $24 - 36n$ ....

c) $n^2 + 6n + 5$ ....   d) $n^2 - 64$ ....

e) $n^2 - 3n - 4$ ....

(5 marks)

Score   / 13

Answer all parts of the questions. Show your workings (on a separate sheet of paper if necessary) and include the correct units in your answers.

1 $a = \sqrt{c - 9}$

Make c the subject of the formula.

(2 marks)

2 a) Expand and simplify $3(2x + 1) - 2(x - 2)$

(2 marks)

b) i) Factorise $6a + 12$

(1 mark)

ii) Factorise completely $10a^2 - 15ab$

(2 marks)

c) i) Factorise $n^2 + 5n + 6$

(2 marks)

ii) Hence simplify fully $\dfrac{2(n + 3)}{n^2 + 5n + 6}$

(2 marks)

d) Factorise fully $(x + y)^2 - 2(x + y)$

(2 marks)

3 Show that $(n - 1)^2 + n + (n - 1)$ simplifies to n^2.

(3 marks)

4 Simplify fully $\dfrac{x^2 - 8x}{x^2 - 9x + 8}$

(3 marks)

5 A person's body mass index (BMI), b, is calculated using the formula:

$$b = \frac{m}{h^2}$$

where m is the person's mass in kilograms and h is their height in metres.

A person is classed as overweight if their BMI is greater than 25. Peter has a height of 184cm and a weight of 89.5kg. Would Peter be classed as overweight? You must show working to justify your answer. 🖩

(3 marks)

Score   / 22

Algebra

How well did you do?

| 0–13 | Try again | 14–18 | Getting there | 19–30 | Good work | 31–40 | Excellent! |

For more information on this topic, see pages 50–53 and 60–61 of your Success Revision Guide.

Equations

Multiple-choice questions

Choose just one answer, a, b, c or d. Circle your choice.

1 Solve the equation $4n - 2 = 10$

    a) $n = 4$ **b)** $n = 2$ **c)** $n = 3$ **d)** $n = 3.5$

2 Solve the equation $4(x + 3) = 16$

    a) $x = 9$ **b)** $x = 7$ **c)** $x = 4$ **d)** $x = 1$

3 Solve the equation $4(n + 2) = 8(n - 3)$

    a) $n = 16$ **b)** $n = 8$ **c)** $n = 4$ **d)** $n = 12$

4 Solve the equation $10 - 6n = 4n - 5$

    a) $n = 2$ **b)** $n = -2$ **c)** $n = 1.5$ **d)** $n = -1.5$

5 Solve the equation $2x^2 - x - 3 = 0$

    a) $x = \frac{3}{2}, x = 1$ **b)** $x = \frac{2}{3}, x = -1$ **c)** $x = \frac{3}{2}, x = -1$ **d)** $x = \frac{2}{3}, x = 1$

U2 | U3

(1 mark)

(1 mark)

(1 mark)

(1 mark)

(1 mark)

Score   / 5

Short-answer questions

Answer all parts of each question.

1 Solve the following equations.

    a) $5n = 25$ **b)** $\frac{n}{3} = 12$

    c) $2n - 4 = 10$ **d)** $3 - 2n = 14$

    e) $\frac{n}{5} + 2 = 7$ **f)** $4 - \frac{n}{2} = 2$

U2 | U3

(6 marks)

2 Solve the following equations.

    a) $12n + 5 = 3n + 32$ **b)** $5n - 4 = 3n + 6$

    c) $5(n + 1) = 25$ **d)** $4(n - 2) = 3(n + 2)$

(4 marks)

3 Solve the following equations.

    a) $n^2 - 4n = 0$ **b)** $n^2 + 6n + 5 = 0$

    c) $n^2 - 5n + 6 = 0$ **d)** $n^2 - 3n - 28 = 0$

(4 marks)

4 The angles in a triangle add up to 180˚. Form an equation in terms of n and solve it.

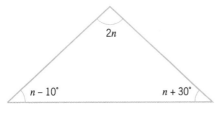

$n =$

(2 marks)

Score   / 16

Answer all parts of the questions. Show your workings (on a separate sheet of paper if necessary) and include the correct units in your answers.

1 Solve these equations.   U2 U3

   a) $5m - 3 = 12$ $m =$ _____   (2 marks)

   b) $8p + 3 = 9 - 2p$ $p =$ _____   (2 marks)

   c) $5(x - 1) = 3x + 7$ $x =$ _____   (2 marks)

   d) $\frac{w}{2} + \frac{(3w + 2)}{3} = \frac{1}{3}$ $w =$ _____   (2 marks)

2 a) Solve $7y - 2 = 3y + 6$

   _____   (2 marks)

   b) Solve $5y + 2 = 2(y - 4)$

   _____   (2 marks)

3 The width of a rectangle is y centimetres. The length of the rectangle is 2 centimetres more than the width. The perimeter of the rectangle is 64 centimetres. Work out the length of the rectangle.

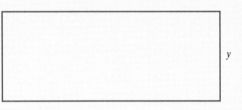

   _____   (4 marks)

4 Solve the equation $x^2 - 4x + 3 = 0$

   $x =$ _____   and $x =$ _____   (3 marks)

5 The diagram shows an irregular pentagon.

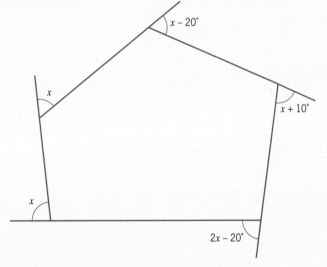

Work out the size of the largest exterior angle.

   _____   (3 marks)

Score   / 22

Algebra

For more information on this topic, see pages 54–55 of your Success Revision Guide.

Equations & inequalities

Multiple-choice questions

Choose just one answer, a, b, c or d. Circle your choice.

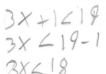

(handwritten working)
$3x + 1 < 19$
$3x < 19 - 1$
$3x < 18$
$x = \frac{18}{3}$

1 Solve the inequality $3x + 1 < 19$

    a) $x < 3$ **b)** $x < 7$ **c)** $x < 5$ **d)** $x < 6$ *(circled)*

    (U2)   (1 mark)

2 Solve the inequality $2x - 7 < 9$ $2x < 16$

    a) $x < 9$ **b)** $x < 10$ **c)** $x < 8$ *(circled)*   **d)** $x < 6.5$

    (1 mark)

3 Solve these simultaneous equations to find the values of a and b.
$a + b = 10$
$2a - b = 2$

    a) $a = 4, b = 6$ **b)** $a = 4, b = -2$ **c)** $a = 5, b = 5$ **d)** $a = 3, b = 7$

    (1 mark)

4 Solve these simultaneous equations to find the values of x and y.
$3x - y = 7$
$2x + y = 3$

    a) $x = 3, y = 2$ **b)** $x = 2, y = 1$ **c)** $x = -3, y = 2$ **d)** $x = 2, y = -1$

    (1 mark)

5 The equation $y^3 + 2y = 82$ has a solution between 4 and 5. By using a method of trial and improvement, find the solution to 1 decimal place. 🖩

    a) 3.9   **b)** 4.1   **c)** 4.2   **d)** 4.3

    (U3)   (1 mark)

Score   / 5

Short-answer questions

Answer all parts of each question.

1 Solve the following inequalities.

    a) $5x + 2 < 12$ _____   **b)** $\frac{x}{3} + 1 \geqslant 3$ _____

    c) $3 \leqslant 2x + 1 \leqslant 9$ _____   **d)** $3 < 3x + 2 \leqslant 8$ _____

    (U2)   (4 marks)

2 Solve these simultaneous equations to find the values of a and b.

    a) $2a + b = 8$
        $3a - b = 2$ $a =$ _____ $b =$ _____

    (2 marks)

    b) $5a + b = 24$
        $2a + 2b = 24$ $a =$ _____ $b =$ _____

    (2 marks)

    c) $4a + 3b = 6$
        $2a - 3b = 12$ $a =$ _____ $b =$ _____

    (2 marks)

3 Use a trial and improvement method to solve the following equation, finding two possible solutions. Give your answer to 1 decimal place. 🖩

    $t^2 - 2t = 20$ $t =$ _____   and $t =$ _____

    (U3)   (2 marks)

Score   / 12

Algebra

Answer all parts of the questions. Show your workings (on a separate sheet of paper if necessary) and include the correct units in your answers.

1 n is an integer. U2

   a) Write down the integer values of n that satisfy the inequality $-4 < n \leqslant 2$

   _____ (2 marks)

   b) Solve the inequality $5p - 2 \leqslant 8$

   _____ (2 marks)

2 The region R satisfies the inequalities:

   $x \geqslant 1$ $\qquad\qquad$ $y \geqslant 2$ $\qquad\qquad$ $x + y \leqslant 8$

   On the grid below, draw straight lines and use shading to show the region R.

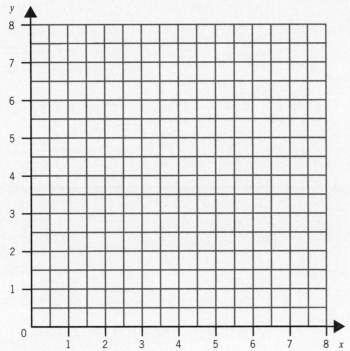

(3 marks)

3 Solve these simultaneous equations.

   $3x - 2y = -12$ $\qquad$ $2x + 6y = 3$ $\qquad$ $x =$ _____ $\qquad$ $y =$ _____ (4 marks)

4 The Gray family, Mr and Mrs Gray and their three children, pay £45 to get into a zoo. The Khan family, Mr and Mrs Khan, their grown-up son and four children, pay £63.75 to get into the zoo. How much are adult and child tickets for the zoo?

   _____ (4 marks)

5 Use the method of trial and improvement to solve the equation $x^3 + 3x = 28$
   Give your answer correct to 1 decimal place. You must show all your working. U3

   _____ (4 marks)

Score   / 19

How well did you do?

0–11 **Try again** $\quad$ 12–21 **Getting there** $\quad$ 22–29 **Good work** $\quad$ 30–36 **Excellent!**

For more information on this topic, see pages 56–58 of your Success Revision Guide.

Multiple-choice questions

Choose just one answer, a, b, c or d. Circle your choice.

1 What are the solutions of the quadratic equation $x^2 - 4 = 0$?

   a) $x = 2, x = 2$ **b)** $x = -2, x = -2$ **c)** $x = 0, x = 4$ **d)** $x = 2, x = -2$

   (U2 | U3)

   (1 mark)

2 What are the solutions of the quadratic equation $6x^2 + 2x = 8$?

   a) $x = 1, x = \frac{3}{4}$ **b)** $x = 1, x = -\frac{4}{3}$ **c)** $x = -1, x = \frac{4}{3}$ **d)** $x = -1, x = -\frac{3}{4}$

   (1 mark)

3 The expression $x^2 + 4x + 7$ is written in the form $(x + a)^2 + b$
What are the values of a and b?

   a) $a = 3, b = 6$ **b)** $a = 4, b = -3$ **c)** $a = 2, b = 3$ **d)** $a = 4, b = 2$

   (1 mark)

4 The expression $x^2 - 2x + 3$ is written in the form $(x + a)^2 + b$
What are the values of a and b?

   a) $a = 1, b = 2$ **b)** $a = -1, b = -2$ **c)** $a = -1, b = 2$ **d)** $a = 1, b = -2$

   (1 mark)

5 What are the solutions of the quadratic equation $2x^2 + 5x + 2 = 0$?

   a) $x = -\frac{1}{2}, x = -2$ **b)** $x = \frac{1}{2}, x = -2$ **c)** $x = -\frac{1}{2}, x = 2$ **d)** $x = 2, x = -2$

   (1 mark)

Score   / 5

Short-answer questions

Answer all parts of each question.

1 The formula $a = \dfrac{3(b + c)}{bc}$ is rearranged to make c the subject. Greg says the answer is
$c = \dfrac{3b}{ab - 3}$

Decide whether Greg is right. You must justify your answer.

   (U2)

   (3 marks)

2 a) Factorise $x^2 + 11x + 30$ **(2 marks)**

   b) Write the following as a single fraction in its simplest form.

   $\dfrac{4}{x + 6} + \dfrac{4}{x^2 + 11x + 30}$

   (U2 | U3)

   (4 marks)

3 $(x + 4)(x - 3) = 2$

   a) Show that $x^2 + x - 14 = 0$

   (2 marks)

   b) Solve the equation $x^2 + x - 14 = 0$
   Give your answer correct to 3 significant figures. 🖩

   (3 marks)

Score   / 14

Algebra

Answer all parts of the questions. Show your workings (on a separate sheet of paper if necessary) and include the correct units in your answers.

1 Make b the subject of the formula $a = \dfrac{8b + 5}{4 - 3b}$

(U2)

(4 marks)

2 Make y the subject of the formula $a(y - b) = a^3 + by$

(3 marks)

3 The expression $x^2 + 6x + 3$ can be written in the form $(x + a)^2 + b$ for all values of x.

(U2)(U3)

a) Find a and b.

$a =$ ....

$b =$ ....

(3 marks)

b) The expression $x^2 + 6x + 3$ has a minimum value. Use your answer to part a) to find this minimum value.

(1 mark)

4 Solve $\dfrac{4}{2x - 1} - \dfrac{1}{x + 1} = 1$ ....

(6 marks)

5 The diagram shows a right-angled triangle with base $(x - 3)$ and height $(x + 4)$. All measurements are in centimetres. The area of the triangle is 12 square centimetres.

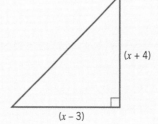

$(x + 4)$

$(x - 3)$

a) Show that $x^2 + x - 36 = 0$ ▦

(3 marks)

b) Find the length of the base of the triangle. Give your answer correct to 2 decimal places. ▦

.... cm

(4 marks)

6 Anna is using the quadratic formula to solve a quadratic equation. After substituting the values she writes $x = \dfrac{5 \pm \sqrt{25 - 36}}{6}$

a) What is the quadratic equation Anna is trying to solve?

(3 marks)

b) Explain why Anna will not be able to find any solutions to the equation.

(1 mark)

Score   / 28

Algebra

For more information on this topic, see pages 50–53 and 60–62 of your Success Revision Guide.

Direct & inverse proportion

Multiple-choice questions

Choose just one answer, a, b, c or d. Circle your choice.

1 If a is directly proportional to b and $a = 10$ when $b = 5$, what is the formula that connects a and b?

U3

    a) $a = 5b$ **b)** $a = 10b$ **c)** $a = \frac{1}{2}b$ **d)** $a = 2b$ **(1 mark)**

2 If y is directly proportional to x and $y = 12$ when $x = 4$, what is the formula that connects x and y?

    a) $y = 3x$ **b)** $x = 3y$ **c)** $y = 12x$ **d)** $y = \frac{1}{3x}$ **(1 mark)**

3 If d is inversely proportional to c, so that $d = \frac{k}{c}$, what is the value of k when $d = 6$ and $c = 3$?

    a) 12   **b)** 18   **c)** 2   **d)** 9   **(1 mark)**

4 If v is inversely proportional to w^2 and $v = 3$ when $w = 2$, what is the formula that connects v and w^2?

    a) $v = \frac{18}{w^2}$ **b)** $v = \frac{2}{w^2}$ **c)** $v = \frac{12}{w^2}$ **d)** $v = \frac{3}{2w^2}$ **(1 mark)**

Score   / 4

Short-answer questions

Answer all parts of each question.

1 The variables x and y are related so that y is directly proportional to the square of x. Complete this table for values of x and y.

U3

x	2	4		
y	12		27	75

(3 marks)

2 z is inversely proportional to the square of v.

    a) Express z in terms of v and a constant of proportionality k.

    (2 marks)

    b) If $z = 10$ when $v = 5$, calculate:

      i) the value of z when $v = 2$ **(2 marks)**

      ii) the value of v when $z = 1000$ **(2 marks)**

3 a is directly proportional to b. $a = 40$ when $b = 5$.

Calculate the value of a when $b = 12$.   **(2 marks)**

Score   / 11

Success

Success

AQA
GCSE Mathematics
Higher
Workbook Answers

Answers

Answers

Statistics and probability

Page 6 – Collecting data

Multiple-choice questions
1. b
2. a
3. d

Short-answer questions
1. The tick boxes overlap. Which box would somebody who did 2 hours of homework tick?
   It also needs extra boxes for more than 4 hours.
   How much time do you spend, doing homework each night?

0 up to 1 hour	1 up to 2 hours	2 up to 3 hours	3 up to 4 hours	4 up to 5 hours	5 hours or more

2.

Year group	Number of students	Number of students in sample
7	120	15
8	176	22
9	160	20
10	190	24
11	154	19

GCSE-style questions
1. a) The question is too vague – what is meant by a healthy diet? The tick options are too vague – how often is 'sometimes'? And 'every day' and 'yes' could mean the same.
   b) Method 1, since all the patients have an equally likely chance of being chosen and this will avoid bias.
2. **The key to this question is to break it into subgroups.**
   On average, how many hours per school day do you spend watching television?
   0 up to 1 hour ☐
   1 up to 2 hours ☐
   2 up to 3 hours ☐
   3 up to 4 hours ☐
   More than 4 hours ☐
   On average, how many hours at the weekend do you spend watching television?
   0 up to 2 hours ☐
   2 up to 4 hours ☐
   4 up to 6 hours ☐
   6 up to 8 hours ☐
   More than 8 hours ☐
3. a) 30 students
   b) 14 girls

Page 8 – Scatter graphs & correlation

Multiple-choice questions
1. c
2. a
3. b

Short-answer questions
1. a) Positive correlation
   b) Negative correlation
   c) Positive correlation
   d) No correlation
2. a) Positive correlation
   b)

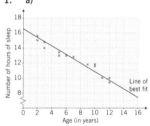

   c) Approximately 72%

GCSE-style questions
1. a)

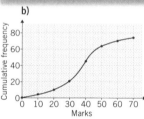

   b) Negative correlation – the younger the child, the more hours of sleep they needed.
   c) See line of best fit on diagram above.
   d) A 4-year-old child has approximately 14 hours of sleep.
   e) This only gives an estimate as it follows the trend of the data. Similarly, if you continued the line it would assume that you may eventually need no hours of sleep at a certain age, which is not the case.
   f) The child psychologist is not correct. From the data, 5-year-old children have approximately 13 hours of sleep.

Page 10 – Averages 1

Multiple-choice questions
1. c
2. b
3. d
4. d

Short-answer questions
1. a) False
   b) True
   c) False
   d) True
2. a) Mean = 141.35
   b) The manufacturer is justified in making this claim because the mean is just over 141, and the mode and median are also approximately 141.
3. $x = 17$

GCSE-style questions
1. a) 5
   b) 3
   c) 4.65
2. 81
3. £440
4. Girls' range = 11; Girls' mean score = 13.4 Conclusion: Boys are better as their mean is higher and the ranges are about the same. Or: There is no difference as the mean and ranges are about the same.

Page 12 – Averages 2

Multiple-choice questions
1. c
2. b
3. a
4. a

Short-answer questions
1. 21.5mm
2. a) 47
   b) 35
   c) 40

GCSE-style questions
1. a) 1 | 2 4 9 5 7 5 8 8
      2 | 2 7 3 5 7 7
      3 | 1 6 5 2 8
      4 | 1
      Reordering gives this:
      1 | 2 4 5 5 7 8 8 9
      2 | 2 3 5 7 7 7
      3 | 1 2 5 6 8
      4 | 1
      Key: 1|2 means 12
   b) 24 minutes
2. a) £31.80
   b) This is only an estimate because the midpoints of the data have been used.
   c) $30 \leqslant x < 40$
   d) Although the modal class interval is $10 \leqslant x < 20$, since the mean is £31.80 and the median class interval is $30 \leqslant x < 40$, Edward's claim is not correct because the other averages indicate that the average amount spent is between £30 and £40.

Page 14 – Cumulative frequency graphs

Multiple-choice questions
1. c
2. d
3. a

Short-answer questions
1. a)

Examination mark	Frequency	Cumulative frequency
0–10	4	4
11–20	6	10
21–30	11	21
31–40	24	45
41–50	18	63
51–60	7	70
61–70	3	73

   b)

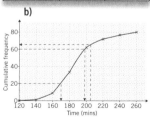

   c) 43 – 27 = 16 marks
   d) 45.5 marks

GCSE-style questions
1. a)

Time (minutes)	Frequency	Cumulative frequency
$120 < t \leqslant 140$	1	1
$140 < t \leqslant 160$	8	9
$160 < t \leqslant 180$	24	33
$180 < t \leqslant 200$	29	62
$200 < t \leqslant 220$	10	72
$220 < t \leqslant 240$	5	77
$240 < t \leqslant 260$	3	80

   b)

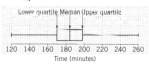

   c) i) Interquartile range = 198 – 170 = 28 minutes
      ii) 80 – 65 = 15 runners
   d)

e) In the second marathon the median time was lower – 160 minutes compared to 185 minutes – and the interquartile range was smaller – 26 minutes as opposed to 28 minutes. All the runners had completed the marathon in 220 minutes or less as opposed to 260 minutes in the first marathon.

Page 16 – Histograms

Multiple-choice questions
1. d
2. b
3. b
4. a

Short-answer questions
1. a)

Time (minutes)	Frequency
$0 < t \leqslant 5$	19
$5 < t \leqslant 15$	**26**
$15 < t \leqslant 20$	16
$20 < t \leqslant 30$	**14**
$30 < t \leqslant 45$	12

b)

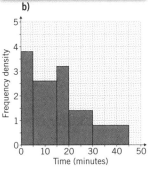

GCSE-style questions
1.

2.

Time (seconds)	Frequency
$0 \leqslant S < 10$	**2**
$10 \leqslant S < 15$	**5**
$15 \leqslant S < 20$	21
$20 \leqslant S < 40$	**28**
$S \geqslant 40$	0

Page 18 – Probability

Multiple-choice questions
1. d
2. c
3. b
4. a
5. d

Short-answer questions
1. a) $\frac{4}{16} = \frac{1}{4}$
   b) $\frac{2}{16} = \frac{1}{8}$
   c) 0
2. 0.09
3. a) $\frac{7}{26}$
   b) $\frac{7}{13}$

GCSE-style questions
1. a) i) 0.35
   ii) 0
   b) 50 times
2. a) $\frac{6}{36} = \frac{1}{6}$
   b) $\frac{4}{36} = \frac{1}{9}$
3. a)

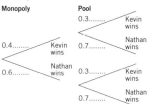

   b) 0.42
   c) 0.46

Number

Page 20 – Fractions

Multiple-choice questions
1. a
2. c
3. b
4. c
5. a

Short-answer questions
1. a) $\frac{1}{7}$ $\frac{3}{10}$ $\frac{1}{2}$ $\frac{2}{3}$ $\frac{3}{4}$ $\frac{4}{5}$
   b) $\frac{1}{9}$ $\frac{2}{7}$ $\frac{1}{3}$ $\frac{2}{5}$ $\frac{5}{8}$ $\frac{3}{4}$
2. a) $\frac{5}{9}$
   b) $\frac{17}{44}$
   c) $\frac{3}{14}$
   d) 3
   e) $1\frac{2}{3}$
   f) $\frac{5}{9}$
   g) $\frac{7}{8}$
   h) $2\frac{34}{49}$
3. a) True
   b) False
4. 28 students

GCSE-style questions
1. a) $1\frac{7}{15}$
   b) $1\frac{16}{33}$
   c) $\frac{8}{63}$
   d) $\frac{3}{4}$
2. $\frac{4}{15}$
3. $\frac{7}{15}$ and £434
4. 7 weeks
5. $\frac{1}{4} + \frac{1}{6} = \frac{6}{24} + \frac{4}{24} = \frac{10}{24}$
   $\frac{10}{24} \times \frac{1}{2} = \frac{5}{24}$
   $\frac{5}{24}$ is not equivalent to $\frac{1}{5}$
6. 22 years

Page 22 – Approximations & checking calculations

Multiple-choice questions
1. d
2. c
3. c
4. b
5. d

Short-answer questions
1. a) 100
   b) 90
2. a) True
   b) False
   c) False
   d) True
3. a) 365
   b) 10.2
   c) 6320
   d) 0.0812

GCSE-style questions
1. a) Vinson Massif and Cartstensz Pyramid.
   b) Yes. Gareth is correct because Mt Everest = 8900 to 2 s.f. and Carstensz = 4900 to 2 s.f. 8900 – 4900 = 4000m.
2. a) 5.937 102
   b) $\frac{30 \times 6}{40 - 10} = \frac{180}{30} = 6$
3. a) 295.390 304 9
   b) 295
4. 7.09 (3 s.f.)
5. 4.5

Page 24 – Percentages 1

Multiple-choice questions
1. d
2. c
3. c
4. a
5. b

Short-answer questions
1. £20
2. £225
3. a) £12
   b) £45
   c) £4
   d) 5g
4. £26 265
5. 39.3% (3 s.f.)
6. 77.3% (1 d.p.)
7. 40%

GCSE-style questions
1. 20%
2. £70
3. 12% reduction
4. a) £30.63
   b) £339.15
5. £36.75

Page 26 – Percentages 2

Multiple-choice questions
1. d
2. a
3. c
4. b

Short-answer questions
1. £515.88
2. £6969.60
3. £135 475.20
4. 121.77p
5. £168.03
6. £75.60

GCSE-style questions
1. £1337.11
2. a) 3.5%
   b) £757.12
3. William will receive £3.20 more interest with Nest Egg.
4. a) 4.5%
   b) £59 728.23
5. £11 340
6. Sale price is 80% of the original price. Terrific Tuesday is 20% of 80% = 64% not 60%.

Page 28 – Fractions, decimals & percentages

Multiple-choice questions
1. c
2. b
3. d
4. d
5. a

Short-answer questions
1. Both will give the same answer because increasing by 20% is the same as multiplying by 1.2. Finding 10% then doubling it gives 20%, which when you add it to 40, is the same as increasing £40 by 20%.
2.

Fraction	Decimal	Percentage
$\frac{2}{5}$	**0.4**	**40%**
$\frac{1}{20}$	**0.05**	5%
$\frac{1}{3}$	$0.\dot{3}$	**33.3%**
$\frac{1}{25}$	**0.04**	**4%**
$\frac{1}{4}$	**0.25**	25%
$\frac{1}{8}$	**0.125**	**12.5%**

GCSE-style questions
1. a) Ed's Electricals: £225
   Sheila's Bargains: £217.38
   Gita's TV Shop: £232
   She should buy from Sheila's Bargains and save £14.62 over the most expensive shop.
   b) £200
2. Rosebushes is cheaper because $\frac{1}{4}$ = 25%, which is greater than the offer at Gardens Are Us.

3. $\frac{1}{8}$, 25%, 0.27, $\frac{1}{3}$, $\frac{2}{5}$, 0.571, 72%

4. $\frac{1}{10}$, $\frac{3}{5}$, $\frac{5}{8}$, $\frac{2}{3}$, $\frac{9}{10}$

Page 30 – Recurring decimals & surds

Multiple-choice questions
1. c
2. d
3. a
4. b
5. a

Short-answer questions
1.

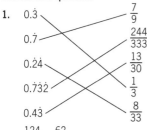

$\dot{0.3}$ — $\frac{7}{9}$
$\dot{0.7}$ — $\frac{244}{333}$
$0.2\dot{4}$ — $\frac{13}{30}$
$0.7\dot{3}\dot{2}$ — $\frac{1}{3}$
$0.4\dot{3}$ — $\frac{8}{33}$

2. $\frac{124}{990} = \frac{62}{495}$

3. a) $2\sqrt{6}$
   b) $5\sqrt{3}$
   c) $6\sqrt{3}$
   d) $6\sqrt{5}$

4. $\frac{3\sqrt{2}}{2}$

GCSE-style questions
1. a) $\frac{6}{11}$
   b) $\frac{26}{990} = \frac{13}{495}$
2. a) 9
   b) $a = 4$
   c) $\frac{3}{5}$
3. a) $\sqrt{60} = \sqrt{4} \times \sqrt{15}$
   $= 2\sqrt{15}$
   b) $(\sqrt{3} + \sqrt{10})^2 =$
   $(\sqrt{3} + \sqrt{10})(\sqrt{3} + \sqrt{10})$
   $= 3 + 2\sqrt{30} + 10$
   $= 13 + 2\sqrt{30}$
   c) $\frac{\sqrt{3}}{3}$
4. $\frac{61}{495}$
5. $19 - 8\sqrt{3}$
6. $\frac{\sqrt{125} + \sqrt{50}}{\sqrt{5}}$
   $\frac{5\sqrt{5} + 5\sqrt{2}}{\sqrt{5}}$
   $\frac{5\sqrt{5} + 5\sqrt{2}}{\sqrt{5}} \times \frac{\sqrt{5}}{\sqrt{5}}$
   $\frac{5(\sqrt{5})^2 + 5\sqrt{10}}{5}$
   $= 5 + \sqrt{10}$
7. $1 + \sqrt{2}$
8. $\frac{25}{33}$
9. $0.4\dot{5} = \frac{5}{11}$
   $x = 0.454545....$
   $100x = 45.454545....$
   $99x = 45$
   $x = \frac{45}{99}$
   $x = \frac{5}{11}$

Page 32 – Ratio

Multiple-choice questions
1. c
2. d
3. d
4. b
5. c

Short-answer questions
1. $1 : 1.5$
2. 1200ml
3. 4.5 days
4. £666.06
5. a) £10.25
   b) 48g
6. £25 000

GCSE-style questions
1. £206
2. Butter: 75g; Sugar: 60g; Eggs: 3; Flour: 67.5g; Milk: 22.5ml
3. 6 days
4. 14 staff
5. Vicky: £6400; Tracy: £8000
6. Small tin cost per gram = $24 \div 142 = 0.169p$
   Large tin cost per gram = $49 \div 300 = 0.16\dot{3}p$
   Therefore, the large tin is the better buy.

Page 34 – Indices

Multiple-choice questions
1. a
2. c
3. d
4. a
5. b

Short-answer questions
1. a) False
   b) False
   c) True
   d) False
   e) False
   f) True
2. a) 1
   b) $16a^8$
   c) $\frac{3}{4}a^{-3}$ or $\frac{3}{4a^3}$
   d) $27a^6b^9$
3. a) $4x^{-2}$
   b) a^2b^{-3}
   c) $3y^{-5}$
4. a) $\pm\frac{1}{5}$
   b) 343
   c) $\frac{25}{16}$
   d) $\frac{1}{27}$

GCSE-style questions
1. Olivia is wrong because
   $m^3 \times m^2 = m^5$.
   $(m \times m \times m) + (m \times m)$.
   You add the powers.
2. a) p^7
   b) n^{-4} or $\frac{1}{n^4}$
   c) a^6
   d) $4ab$

---

3. a) 1
   b) $\frac{1}{81}$
   c) 648
   d) 16
   e) $\frac{1}{5}$
4. a) i) 1
   ii) $\frac{1}{16}$
   iii) $\pm\frac{3}{2} = \pm1\frac{1}{2}$
   b) 5^4
5. a) $\frac{1}{125}$
   b) $\frac{9}{4}$
   c) $\frac{1}{4}$
6. a) $\frac{1}{2}$ or 2^{-1}
   b) 2^{20}
   c) $2^{\frac{5}{2}}$
7. a) $125x^3$
   b) y^{20}
   c) $\frac{1}{27y^3}$ or $\frac{1}{27}y^{-3}$
   d) $32x^5y^{15}$

Page 36 – Standard index form

Multiple-choice questions
1. b
2. b
3. a
4. b
5. b

Short-answer questions
1. a) True
   b) False
   c) False
   d) False
2. a) 8.19×10^3
   b) 7.56×10^2
   c) 6×10^{-7}
3. 1.8×10^{-7} grams
4. a) 8×10^{15}
   b) 1.4×10^4
   c) 3×10^{16}

GCSE-style questions
1. 1.25×10^{-10}
2. 2.6×10^{-6}g
3. 9.3×10^4
4. a) £8.6×10^5
   b) £6.2×10^5
5. a) i) 207 000
   ii) 4.6×10^{-5}
   b) 3.5×10^{12}

Page 38 – Upper & lower bounds of measurement

Multiple-choice questions
1. b
2. c
3. c
4. b
5. d

Short-answer questions
1. 111.5g
2. Lower bound: e
   Upper bound: a
3. $11.25cm^2$

GCSE style questions
1. a) 7.9cm
   b) 0.642cm
2. 0.886m

---

3. The upper bound for Jaydn's petrol consumption is $146.5 \div 15.55 = 9.42$ miles per litre, so Jaydn's claim is almost certainly not correct.
4. Lower bound = 3.9717cm (5 s.f.)
   Upper bound = 3.9738cm (5 s.f.)
5. 0.1811gcm$^{-3} \leqslant$ density < 0.2gcm^{-3}

Algebra

Page 40 – Algebra & formulae

Multiple-choice questions
1. a
2. d
3. c
4. d
5. c

Short-answer questions
1. a) $b = \frac{p + 4}{3}$
   b) $b = \pm\sqrt{4y + 6}$
   c) $b = \frac{2 - 5n}{3}$
2. $T = 6b + 0.67p$ or $600b + 67p$
3. a) 4
   b) 5
   c) ±8
4. a) $5(2n + 3)$
   b) $12(2 - 3n)$
   c) $(n + 1)(n + 5)$
   d) $(n - 8)(n + 8)$
   e) $(n + 1)(n - 4)$

GCSE-style questions
1. $c = a^2 + 9$
2. a) $4x + 7$
   b) i) $6(a + 2)$
   ii) $5a(2a - 3b)$
   c) i) $(n + 2)(n + 3)$
   ii) $\frac{2}{n + 2}$
   d) $(x + y)(x + y - 2)$
3. $(n - 1)^2 + n + (n - 1)$
   $= n^2 - 2n + 1 + n + n - 1$
   $= n^2 - 2n + 1 + 2n - 1$
   $= n^2$
4. $\frac{x^2 - 8x}{x^2 - 9x + 8} = \frac{x(x - 8)}{(x - 8)(x - 1)}$
   $= \frac{x}{(x - 1)}$
5. BMI = 26.4 (3 s.f.) so Peter is classed as overweight.

Page 42 – Equations

Multiple-choice questions
1. c
2. d
3. b
4. c
5. c

Short-answer questions
1. a) $n = 5$
   b) $n = 36$
   c) $n = 7$
   d) $n = -5.5$
   e) $n = 25$
   f) $n = 4$
2. a) $n = 3$
   b) $n - 5$
   c) $n = 4$
   d) $n = 14$

3. a) $n = 0$, $n = 4$
  b) $n = -5$, $n = -1$
  c) $n = 3$, $n = 2$
  d) $n = -4$, $n = 7$
4. $2n + (n + 30°) + (n - 10°) = 180°$
  $4n + 20° = 180°$
  $n = 40°$

GCSE-style questions
1. a) $m = 3$
  b) $p = \frac{6}{10}$ or $p = \frac{3}{5}$ or $p = 0.6$
  c) $x = 6$
  d) $\frac{3w + 2(3w + 2)}{6} = \frac{1}{3}$
   $3w + 6w + 4 = \frac{6}{3}$
   $3w + 6w + 4 = 2$
   $9w + 4 = 2$
   $w = -\frac{2}{9}$
2. a) $y = 2$
  b) $y = -\frac{10}{3}$ or $-3\frac{1}{3}$ or $-3.\dot{3}$
3. Length = 17cm
4. $x = 1$ and $x = 3$
5. 110°

Page 44 – Equations & inequalities

Multiple-choice questions
1. d
2. c
3. a
4. d
5. c

Short-answer questions
1. a) $x < 2$
  b) $x \geqslant 6$
  c) $1 \leqslant x \leqslant 4$
  d) $\frac{1}{3} < x \leqslant 2$
2. a) $a = 2$, $b = 4$
  b) $a = 3$, $b = 9$
  c) $a = 3$, $b = -2$
3. $t = 5.6$ and $t = -3.6$

GCSE-style questions
1. a) -3, -2, -1, 0, 1, 2
  b) $p \leqslant 2$
2.

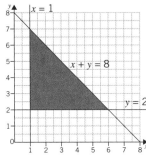

3. $x = -3$, $y = 1.5$
4. Adult = £11.25; Child = £7.50
5. $x = 2.7$

Page 46 – Advanced algebra & equations

Multiple-choice questions
1. d
2. b
3. c
4. c
5. a

Short-answer questions
1. $a = \frac{3(b + c)}{bc}$
  $abc = 3b + 3c$
  $abc - 3c = 3b$
  $c(ab - 3) = 3b$
  Therefore $c = \frac{3b}{ab - 3}$
  Greg is right.
2. a) $(x + 6)(x + 5)$
  b) $\frac{4}{(x + 6)} + \frac{4}{(x^2 + 11x + 30)}$
   $= \frac{4}{(x + 6)} + \frac{4}{(x + 6)(x + 5)}$
   $= \frac{4(x + 5) + 4}{(x + 6)(x + 5)}$
   $= \frac{4x + 24}{(x + 6)(x + 5)}$
   $= \frac{4(x + 6)}{(x + 6)(x + 5)}$
   $= \frac{4}{(x + 5)}$
3. a) $(x + 4)(x - 3) = 2$
   $x^2 + x - 12 = 2$
   $x^2 + x - 14 = 0$
  b) $x = 3.27$ or $x = -4.27$

GCSE-style questions
1. $a = \frac{8b + 5}{(4 - 3b)}$
  $a(4 - 3b) = 8b + 5$
  $4a - 3ab = 8b + 5$
  $4a - 5 = 8b + 3ab$
  $4a - 5 = b(8 + 3a)$
  $b = \frac{4a - 5}{8 + 3a}$
2. $y = \frac{a(a^2 + b)}{(a - b)}$
3. a) $a = 3$, $b = -6$
  b) Minimum value is -6.
4. $x = 2$, $x = -1.5$
5. a) $\frac{1}{2} \times (x - 3) \times (x + 4) = 12$
   $(x - 3)(x + 4) = 24$
   $x^2 + x - 12 = 24$
   $x^2 + x - 36 = 0$
  b) $x = 5.52$ ∴ base of triangle is 2.52cm.
6. a) $3x^2 - 5x + 3 = 0$
  b) No solution since $25 - 36 = -11$ and you cannot $\sqrt{-11}$.

Page 48 – Direct & inverse proportion

Multiple-choice questions
1. d
2. a
3. b
4. c

Short-answer questions
1.

x	2	4	3	5
y	12	48	27	75

2. a) $z = \frac{k}{v^2}$
  b) i) 62.5
   ii) $\pm\frac{1}{2}$
3. 96

GCSE-style questions
1. 9.6
2. $E = kF$
  $6 = k \times 15$
  $\therefore k = \frac{2}{5}$
  $E = \frac{2}{5}F$
  When $F = 80N$, $E = 32cm$
3. $V = kh^3$
  $60 = k \times 8$
  $k = 7.5$
  $V = 7.5h^3$
  $V = 937.5cm^3$
4. a) $I = \frac{k}{d^2}$
   $50 = \frac{k}{4}$
   $\therefore k = 200$
   $I = \frac{200}{d^2}$
   $I = 16.3$
  b) $d = 4$
5. $f = \frac{k}{w}$
  $45 = \frac{k}{16.2}$
  $k = 729$
  $f = \frac{729}{w}$
  $w = \frac{729}{24}$
  $w = 30.375m$
6. $c = \frac{k}{b}$
  $\therefore 4 = \frac{k}{10}$ so $k = 40$
  Daisy is correct.

Page 50 – Linear graphs

Multiple-choice questions
1. b
2. d
3. b
4. c
5. a

Short-answer questions
1. a) and b) i)

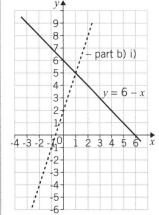

   ii) $y = 3x + 2$
  c) (1, 5)
2. $y = 3 - 2x$ and $y = 4 - 2x$

GCSE-style questions
1. a) Gradient $= -\frac{2}{3}$
  b) $3y + 2x = 6$ or $y = -\frac{2}{3}x + 2$
  c)

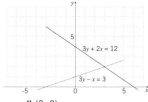

  d) (3, 2)
  e) Amara is correct – the gradient of the line $3y - x = 3$ is $\frac{1}{3}$

Page 52 – Non-linear graphs

Multiple-choice questions
1. b
2. d
3. c
4. d
5. b

Short-answer questions
1. a)

x	-2	-1	0	1	2	3
y	6	1	-2	-3	-2	1

  b)

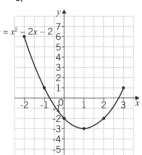

  c) i) $y = -3$
   ii) $x = 2.75$ and $x = -0.75$

GCSE-style questions
1. a)

x	-2	-1	0	1	2	3
y	-12	-5	-4	-3	4	23

  b)

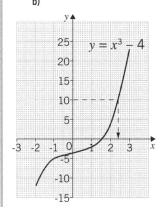

c) i) $x = 1.6$
   ii) $x = 2.4$
   iii) $x = 1.8$
   iv) $x = -1.4$
d) $x = -1.9$ (1 d.p.)

Page 54 – Advanced graphs

Multiple-choice questions
1. c
2. a
3. d
4. c

Short-answer questions
1. Statement is true since $x = -1$, $y = -3$ is a simultaneous solution of the two equations: i.e. $-3 = 2 \times -1 - 1$ and $(-3)^2 = 4 \times -1 + 13$
2. a) $(2, 4)$
   b) $(1, 7)$
   c) $(6, 7)$
   d) $(-2, 7)$
   e) $(1, 7)$

GCSE-style questions
1. a) $x = -1$, $y = 3$
      $x = 4$, $y = 8$
   b) They are the coordinates of the points where the line $y = x + 4$ intersects with the graph $y = x^2 - 2x$.
2. a)

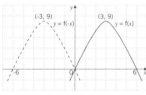

   b)

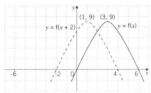

3. $y = f(x + 6)$

Page 56 – Interpreting graphs

Multiple-choice questions
1. d
2. a
3. d

Short-answer questions
1. Vase A – graph 2
   Vase B – graph 1
   Vase C – graph 3.
2. a) Roots are $x = 3$ and $x = -2$ (read where curve crosses x-axis).
   b) i) Approximately, $x = 3.4$ and $x = -2.4$ (read across where $y = 2$).
      ii) Approximately, $x = -2.7$ and $x = 2.7$ (draw the line $y = 1 - x$ and find the point of intersection with the curve).

GCSE-style questions
GCSE-style questions
1. a)

Equation	Graph
$y - x^2 - x - 6$	D
$y = 6 - x^2$	E
$y = x^3$	F
$y = 3x + 2$	B
$y = 5 - x$	A
$y = \frac{2}{x}$	C

2. $a = 2$, $b = 3$

Geometry and measures

Page 58 – Measures & measurement

Multiple-choice questions
1. a
2. d
3. b
4. d
5. c

Short-answer questions
1. a) 8000m
   b) 3.25kg
   c) 7000kg
   d) 0.52m
   e) 2700ml
   f) 0.002 62km
2. 12.5 miles
3. 1.32 pounds
4. 60mph
5. 0.1g/cm^{-3}

GCSE-style questions
1. Length = 12.05cm
   Width = 5.5cm
2. a) 17.6 pounds
   b) 48km
3. 80kg
4. a) 1 hour 30 minutes = 90 minutes
   b) 5.1km/h
5. Speed = $2400 \div 108$ = $22.\dot{2}$m/s
   $22.\dot{2}$m/s $\div 4.47$ = 4.97
   4.97×10mph = 49.7mph
   The car was not speeding through the roadworks.

Page 60 – Transformations 1

Multiple-choice questions
1. a
2. c
3. b
4. b

Short-answer questions
1. a)–c)

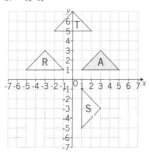

2. a) Translation
   b) Rotation
   c) Translation
   d) Reflection

GCSE-style questions
1. a) Reflection in the x-axis.
   b) Rotation 90° anticlockwise about $(0, 0)$.
2. a)–b)

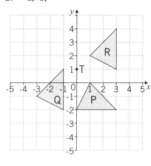

Page 62 – Transformations 2

Multiple-choice questions
1. d
2. b
3. b

Short-answer questions
1. a) Reflection in the y-axis.
   b) Rotation 90° clockwise about $(0, 0)$.
   c) Reflection in the line $y = x$
2.

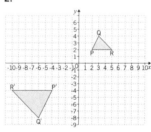

GCSE-style questions
1.

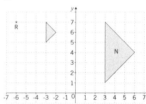

2. a) Translation by the vector $\begin{pmatrix} -12 \\ -7 \end{pmatrix}$
   b) Enlargement by a scale factor of $-\frac{1}{2}$, centre of enlargement at $(0, 5)$.
   c) Reflection in the line $y = 0$ or x-axis.

Page 64 – Bearings & scale drawings

Multiple-choice questions
1. c
2. a
3. d
4. b

Short-answer questions
1. 10km
2. a) Your diagram should have a scale of 1cm to 2km.

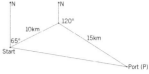

   b) 11.1cm = 22.2km ($\pm$ 0.2km)
   c) 098° (± 1°)
3. False

GCSE-style questions
1. a) 165m
   b) 210°
   c)

   Diagram not accurately drawn
2. Lengths must be ± 2mm.

Page 66 – Loci & coordinates in 3D

Multiple-choice questions
1. c
2. d
3. a
4. d
5. b

Short-answer questions
1.

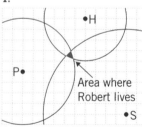

2. $R = (3, 3, 0)$
   $S = (3, 1, 3)$
   $T = (0, 1, 3)$
   $U = (0, 1, 1)$

Answers

GCSE-style questions
1. a)–b)

(Radius 5 cm)

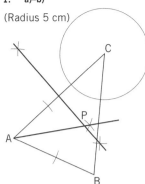

2. (5, 0, 3)

Page 68 – Angle properties of circles

Multiple-choice questions
1. c
2. a
3. d
4. a
5. c

Short-answer questions
1. a) $a = 65°$
   b) $a = 50°$
   c) $a = 18°$
   d) $a = 60°$
   e) $a = 82°$
2. John is correct. Angle a is 42° because angles in the same segment are equal.

GCSE-style questions
1. a) Angle ROQ = 140°
   b) Angle PRQ = 70°
2. Angle A = 63° (alternate segment theorem)
   $p = 180° - 63° - 71°$ (angles in a triangle)
   $p = 46°$
3. Billy is correct since angle OBC = 90° (tangent and radius meet at 90°) hence angle OBA = 90° – y. Since angle OBA = angle OAB, triangle AOB is isosceles.
   ∴ angle AOB = 180° – 2 (90° – y) because angles in a triangle add up to 180°
   = 180° – 180° + 2y
   = 2y

Page 70 – Pythagoras' theorem

Multiple-choice questions
1. d
2. b
3. a
4. c

Short-answer questions
1. a) $n = 15$cm
   b) $n = 12.6$cm
   c) $n = 29.1$cm
   d) $n = 24.6$cm
2. Since $12^2 + 5^2 = 144 + 25 = 169 = 13^2$, the triangle must be right-angled for Pythagoras' theorem to be applied.
3. Both statements are true.
   Length of line = $\sqrt{6^2 + 3^2}$ = $\sqrt{45}$ in surd form.
   Midpoint = $\frac{(2 + 5)}{2}, \frac{(11 + 5)}{2}$
   = (3.5, 8)

GCSE-style questions
1. 13.7m
2. $\sqrt{41}$ units
3. 48.6m
4. £13.52

Page 72 – Trigonometry in right-angled triangles

Multiple-choice questions
1. a
2. b
3. d
4. a
5. c

Short-answer questions
1. a) $n = 5$cm
   b) $n = 6.3$cm
   c) $n = 13.8$cm
   d) $n = 14.9$cm
   e) $n = 6.7$cm
2. a) 38.7°
   b) 52.5°
   c) 23.6°

GCSE-style questions
1. 15cm
2. 65°
3. 62.6cm²
4. 2.7m

Page 74 – Application of trigonometry

Multiple-choice questions
1. c
2. a
3. c
4. b

Short-answer questions
1. 068°
2. 13.8cm (1 d.p.)
3. a) i) True
      ii) True
   b) 40.9° (1 d.p.)

GCSE-style questions
1. 30.1°
2. 206°
3. a) 389.9m
   b) 14.6°
   c) 22.6°

Page 76 – Further trigonometry

Multiple-choice questions
1. c
2. a
3. d
4. c

Short-answer questions
1. a) 13.2cm (3 s.f.)
   b) 17.3cm (3 s.f.)
   c) 32.5° (1 d.p.)
   d) 70.9° (1 d.p.)
2. Area = $\frac{1}{2} \times 18 \times 13 \times \sin 37°$
   = 70.4cm²
   Area is approximately 70cm². Isobel is correct.
3. a) A (0°, 1), B (90°, 0), C (270°, 0), D (360°, 1)
   b)

GCSE-style questions
1. a) 10.5cm
   b) 12.5cm²
   c) 42.5cm²
2. 4.13cm

Page 78 – Area of 2D shapes

Multiple-choice questions
1. c
2. d
3. b
4. d

Short-answer questions
1. a) False
   b) False
   c) False
2. 38.6cm
3. 87.03cm²
4. 70 000cm²

GCSE-style questions
1. £33
2. 363.6cm²
3. 16cm
4. £2170

Page 80 – Volume of 3D shapes

Multiple-choice questions
1. c
2. c
3. d

Short-answer questions
1. Emily is not correct. The correct volume is 345.6 ÷ 2, i.e. 172.8cm³.
2. 170.2m³
3. 9.9cm
4. 3807cm³
5. 156cm²

GCSE-style questions
1. 64cm³
2. a) 672cm³
   b) 3696g or 3.696kg
3. 3.2cm
4. £25.35

Page 82 – Further length, area & volume

Multiple-choice questions
1. b
2. a
3. d
4. a
5. c

Short-answer questions
1. Solid A is 314cm³
   Solid B is 600cm³
   Solid C is 2145cm³
   Solid D is 68cm³
2. The statement is false because:
   Area of segment = area of sector – area of triangle = 13.09 – 10.83 = 2.26cm²

GCSE-style questions
1. 20.1cm
2. 73°
3. 0.0248m³
4. 8mm

Page 84 – Similarity & congruency

Multiple-choice questions
1. c
2. b
3. a
4. b

Short-answer questions
1. a) $n = 8$cm
   b) $n = 6.\dot{6}$cm
   c) $n = 9.8$cm
2. a) Congruent (RHS)
   b) Not congruent
   c) Congruent (SSS)

GCSE-style questions
1. a) 5cm
   b) 15cm
2. a) 450cm²
   b) 1.08 litres
3. RST and RUT are both isosceles triangles.
   Common length is RT
   Angle RST = Angle RUT
   Angle SRT = Angle URT
   Angle UTR = Angle STR
   Since three angles and one side are the same, triangles RST and RUT are congruent.

Page 86 – Vectors

Multiple-choice questions
1. b
2. c
3. a
4. b
5. b

Short-answer questions
1. a) True
   b) False
   c) True
   d) False
2. $\vec{OC} = 2\mathbf{a} - 3\mathbf{b}$,
   $\vec{OD} = 6(2\mathbf{a} - 3\mathbf{b})$
   Hence the vectors are parallel as one vector is a multiple of the other. The vectors lie on a straight line through O.
3.

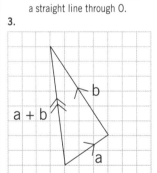

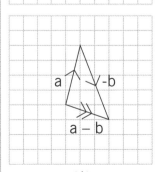

   a) $\mathbf{a} + \mathbf{b} = \begin{pmatrix} -1 \\ 8 \end{pmatrix}$
   b) $\mathbf{a} - \mathbf{b} = \begin{pmatrix} 3 \\ -1 \end{pmatrix}$

GCSE-style questions

1. $\begin{pmatrix} 2 \\ 4 \end{pmatrix}$

2. $\overrightarrow{AB} = -3\mathbf{a} + 3\mathbf{b}$,
   $\overrightarrow{CD} = -5\mathbf{a} + 5\mathbf{b}$
   Since $\overrightarrow{AB} = \frac{3}{5}\overrightarrow{CD}$, AB and CD are parallel.

3. a) $\overrightarrow{AC} = \mathbf{a} + \mathbf{b}$
   b) $\overrightarrow{BD} = \mathbf{b} + 2\mathbf{b} - \mathbf{a}$
   $\phantom{b) \overrightarrow{BD}} = 3\mathbf{b} - \mathbf{a}$
   hence $\overrightarrow{AD} = \overrightarrow{AB} + \overrightarrow{BD}$
   $\phantom{hence \overrightarrow{AD}} = \mathbf{a} + 3\mathbf{b} - \mathbf{a}$
   $\overrightarrow{AD} = 3\mathbf{b}$
   $\overrightarrow{AD} = 3\overrightarrow{BC}$, so BC is parallel to AD.
   c) $\overrightarrow{AN} = \overrightarrow{AD} + \overrightarrow{DN}$
   $\phantom{c) \overrightarrow{AN}} = 3\mathbf{b} - \frac{1}{2}(2\mathbf{b} - \mathbf{a})$
   $\phantom{c) \overrightarrow{AN}} = 3\mathbf{b} - \mathbf{b} + \frac{1}{2}\mathbf{a}$
   $\phantom{c) \overrightarrow{AN}} = \frac{1}{2}\mathbf{a} + 2\mathbf{b}$
   d) $\overrightarrow{YD} = \overrightarrow{YA} + \overrightarrow{AD}$
   $\phantom{d) \overrightarrow{YD}} = -\frac{3}{4}(\frac{1}{2}\mathbf{a} + 2\mathbf{b}) + 3\mathbf{b}$
   $\phantom{d) \overrightarrow{YD}} = -\frac{3}{8}\mathbf{a} - \frac{3}{2}\mathbf{b} + 3\mathbf{b}$
   $\phantom{d) \overrightarrow{YD}} = -\frac{3}{8}\mathbf{a} + \frac{3}{2}\mathbf{b}$
   $\phantom{d) \overrightarrow{YD}} = \frac{3}{8}(4\mathbf{b} - \mathbf{a})$

Published by Letts Educational Ltd.
An imprint of HarperCollins*Publishers*

Text © Fiona Mapp
Design and illustration © 2010 Letts Educational Ltd.

Answer all parts of the questions. Show your workings (on a separate sheet of paper if necessary) and include the correct units in your answers.

1. P is directly proportional to the square root of q when $P = 6$, $q = 25$. Calculate the value of P when $q = 64$. **U3**

_____

(3 marks)

2. The extension (E) of a spring is directly proportional to the force (F) pulling the spring. The extension is 6cm when a force of 15N is pulling it. Calculate the extension when the force is 80N.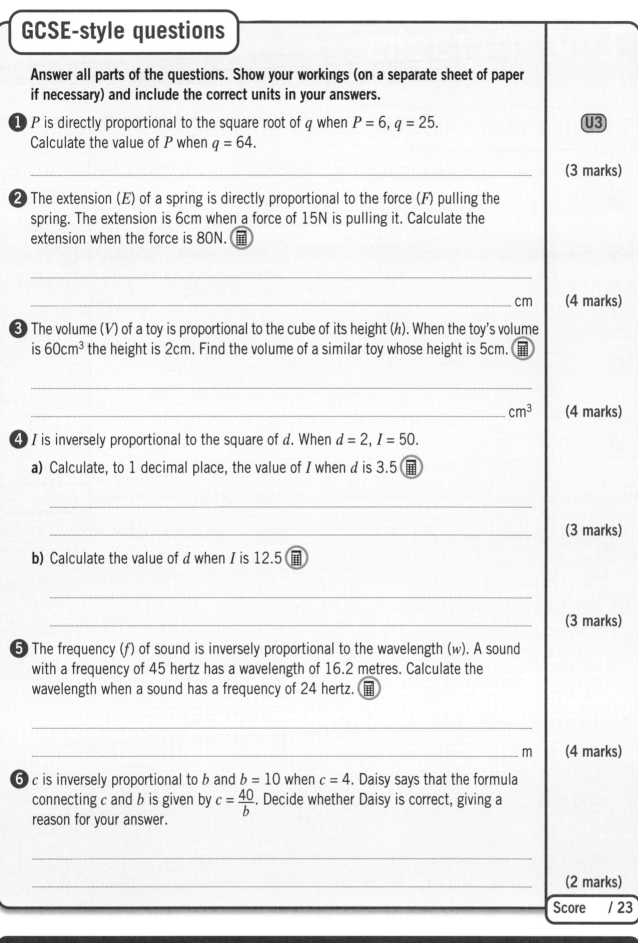

_____

_____ cm   (4 marks)

3. The volume (V) of a toy is proportional to the cube of its height (h). When the toy's volume is 60cm³ the height is 2cm. Find the volume of a similar toy whose height is 5cm.

_____

_____ cm³   (4 marks)

4. I is inversely proportional to the square of d. When $d = 2$, $I = 50$.

   a) Calculate, to 1 decimal place, the value of I when d is 3.5

   _____

   _____

   (3 marks)

   b) Calculate the value of d when I is 12.5

   _____

   _____

   (3 marks)

5. The frequency (f) of sound is inversely proportional to the wavelength (w). A sound with a frequency of 45 hertz has a wavelength of 16.2 metres. Calculate the wavelength when a sound has a frequency of 24 hertz.

_____

_____ m   (4 marks)

6. c is inversely proportional to b and $b = 10$ when $c = 4$. Daisy says that the formula connecting c and b is given by $c = \frac{40}{b}$. Decide whether Daisy is correct, giving a reason for your answer.

_____

_____

(2 marks)

Score   / 23

Algebra

How well did you do?

| 0–8 | Try again | 9–16 | Getting there | 17–28 | Good work | 29–38 | Excellent! |

For more information on this topic, see page 63 of your Success Revision Guide.

49

Linear graphs

Multiple-choice questions

Choose just one answer, a, b, c or d. Circle your choice.

1 Which pair of coordinates lies on the line $x = 2$?

   a) (1, 3)   **b)** (2, 3)   **c)** (3, 2)   **d)** (0, 2)

(U2)

(1 mark)

2 Which pair of coordinates lies on the line $y = -3$?

   a) (-3, 5)   **b)** (5, -2)   **c)** (-2, 5)   **d)** (5, -3)

(1 mark)

3 What is the gradient of the line $y = 2 - 5x$?

   a) -2   **b)** -5   **c)** 2   **d)** 5

(1 mark)

4 These graphs have been drawn: $y = 3x - 1$, $y = 5 - 2x$, $y = 6x + 1$, $y = 2x - 3$
Which graph is the steepest?

   a) $y = 3x - 1$ **b)** $y = 5 - 2x$ **c)** $y = 6x + 1$ **d)** $y = 2x - 3$

(1 mark)

5 At what point does the graph $y = 3x - 4$ intercept the y-axis?

   a) (0, -4)   **b)** (0, 3)   **c)** (-4, 0)   **d)** (3, 0)

(1 mark)

Score   / 5

Short-answer questions

Answer all parts of each question.

1 a) On the grid, draw the graph of $y = 6 - x$.
Join your points with a straight line.

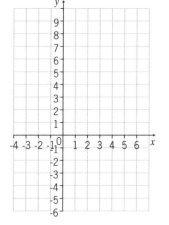

(U2)

(2 marks)

b) A second line goes through the coordinates
(1, 5), (-2, -4) and (2, 8).

   i) Draw this line on the grid.

(1 mark)

   ii) Write down the equation of the line you have just drawn.

_____

(2 marks)

c) What are the coordinates of the point where the two lines intercept?

_____

(1 mark)

2 The equations of five straight lines are: $y = 2x - 4$, $y = 3 - 2x$, $y = 4 - 2x$, $y = 5x - 4$, $y = 3x - 5$. Two of the lines are parallel. Write down the equations of these two lines.

_____ and _____

(2 marks)

Score   / 8

Answer all parts of the questions. Show your workings (on a separate sheet of paper if necessary) and include the correct units in your answers.

1 The line with equation $3y + 2x = 12$ has been drawn on the grid.

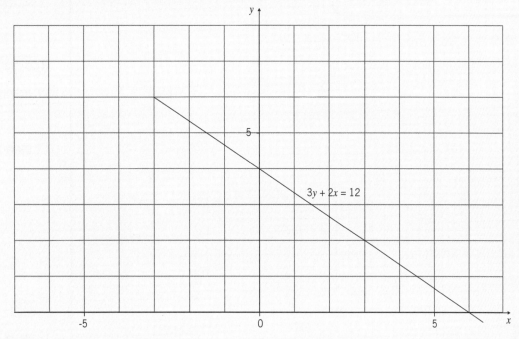

$3y + 2x = 12$

a) Write down the gradient of the line $3y + 2x = 12$

.... (2 marks)

b) Write down the equation of the line that is parallel to $3y + 2x = 12$ and passes through the point with coordinates (0, 2).

.... (1 mark)

c) On the grid above, draw the graph with the equation $3y - x = 3$ (2 marks)

d) Write down the coordinates of the point of intersection of the two straight-line graphs, $3y + 2x = 12$ and $3y - x = 3$

(................, ...) (1 mark)

e) Amara says, 'The line $y = \frac{1}{3}x - 4$ is parallel to the graph $3y - x = 3$'.
Explain whether Amara is correct. Give a reason for your answer.

....

.... (2 marks)

Score   / 8

Algebra

How well did you do?

| 0–4 | Try again | | 5–9 | Getting there | | 10–15 | Good work | | 16–21 | Excellent! |

For more information on this topic, see pages 64–65 of your Success Revision Guide.

Non-linear graphs

Algebra

Multiple-choice questions

Choose just one answer, a, b, c or d. Circle your choice.

1 Which pair of coordinates lies on the graph $y = x^2 - 2$?

a) $(1, 1)$ **b)** $(4, 14)$ **c)** $(2, 4)$ **d)** $(0, 2)$

U2 U3

(1 mark)

2 On which of these curves do the coordinates $(2, 5)$ lie?

a) $y = x^2 - 4$ **b)** $y = 2x^2 + 3$ **c)** $y = x^2 - 6$ **d)** $y = 2x^2 - 3$

(1 mark)

Questions 3–5 refer to these diagrams:

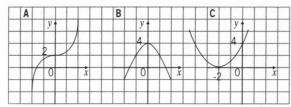

3 What is the equation of graph A?

a) $y = 5 - 2x^2$ **b)** $y = x^2 + 4x + 4$ **c)** $y = x^3 + 2$ **d)** $y = 4 - x^2$

U3

(1 mark)

4 What is the equation of graph B?

a) $y = 5 - 2x^2$ **b)** $y = x^2 + 4x + 4$ **c)** $y = x^3 + 2$ **d)** $y = 4 - x^2$

(1 mark)

5 What is the equation of graph C?

a) $y = 5 - 2x^2$ **b)** $y = x^2 + 4x + 4$ **c)** $y = x^3 + 2$ **d)** $y = 4 - x^2$

(1 mark)

Score   / 5

Short-answer questions

Answer all parts of each question.

1 **a)** Complete the table of values for $y = x^2 - 2x - 2$

U2 U3

x	-2	-1	0	1	2	3
$y = x^2 - 2x - 2$			-2			1

(2 marks)

b) On the grid below, draw the graph of $y = x^2 - 2x - 2$

(3 marks)

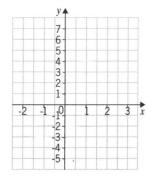

c) Use your graph to write down an estimate for:

   i) the minimum value of y

     $y = $ _____

(1 mark)

   ii) the solutions of the equation $x^2 - 2x - 2 = 0$

     $x = $ _____ and $x = $ _____

(2 marks)

Score   / 8

Answer all parts of the questions. Show your workings (on a separate sheet of paper if necessary) and include the correct units in your answers.

1 **a)** Complete the table of values for the graph $y = x^3 - 4$ 🖩   (U3)

x	-2	-1	0	1	2	3
$y = x^3 - 4$		-5				23

(2 marks)

b) On the grid, draw the graph of $y = x^3 - 4$ for values of x between -2 and 3.

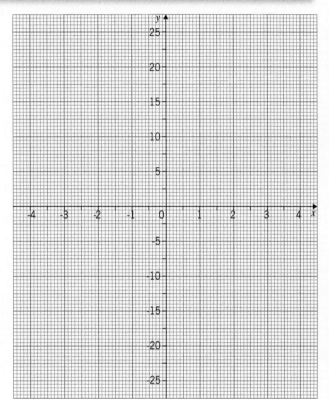

(2 marks)

c) Use your graph to find an estimate of:

i) the solution of the equation $x^3 - 4 = 0$

$x = $ ....   (1 mark)

ii) the solution of the equation $x^3 - 4 = 10$

$x = $ ....   (2 marks)

iii) the solution of the equation $x^3 - 4 = 2$

$x = $ ....   (2 marks)

iv) the solution of the equation $x^3 - 4 = -7$

$x = $ ....   (2 marks)

d) By drawing an appropriate linear graph, solve the equation $x^3 - 2x + 3 = 0$

$x = $ ....   (5 marks)

Score   / 16

Algebra

For more information on this topic, see pages 66–67 of your Success Revision Guide.

Advanced graphs

Multiple-choice questions

Choose just one answer, a, b, c or d. Circle your choice.

1 Solve these simultaneous equations to find values for a and b. $\boxed{\text{U2} \mid \text{U3}}$
$a^2 + b^2 = 13 \qquad 2a + b = 7$

   a) $a = -2, b = 3$ **b)** $a = 3, b = 2$ **c)** $a = 2, b = 3$ **d)** $a = 2, b = -3$ (1 mark)

2 Solve these simultaneous equations to find values for a and b.
$a^2 - b = 3 \qquad 3a + b = 1$

   a) $a = 1, b = -2$ **b)** $a = -1, b = 2$ **c)** $a = -1, b = -2$ **d)** $a = 1, b = 2$ (1 mark)

3 Which of these pairs of coordinates are the points of intersection of the quadratic graph $y = x^2 - 2x - 7$ and the straight line $y = x + 3$?

   a) (8, 5)   **b)** (2, 1)   **c)** (-1, 2)   **d)** (-2, 1)   (1 mark)

4 The graph $y = x^2$ is translated two units to the left. What is the equation of the new curve? $\boxed{\text{U3}}$

   a) $y = (x - 2)^2$ **b)** $y = x^2 + 2$ **c)** $y = (x + 2)^2$ **d)** $y = x^2 - 2$ (1 mark)

Score   / 4

Short-answer questions

Answer all parts of each question.

1 Decide whether this statement is true or false: $\boxed{\text{U2} \mid \text{U3}}$
'The line $y = 2x - 1$ intersects with the graph $y^2 = 4x + 13$ at the point (-1, -3).'
Explain your reasoning.

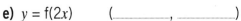

(2 marks)

2 This is a sketch of the curve with the equation $y = \text{f}(x)$. $\boxed{\text{U3}}$
The maximum point of the curve is A (2, 7).
Write down the coordinates of the maximum
point of each of the following curves.

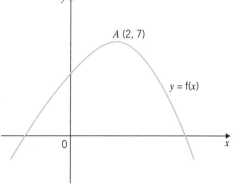

   a) $y = \text{f}(x) - 3$ (............., ...)

   b) $y = \text{f}(x + 1)$ (............., ...)

   c) $y = \text{f}(x - 4)$ (............., ...)

   d) $y = \text{f}(-x)$ (............., ...)

   e) $y = \text{f}(2x)$ (............., ...)

(5 marks)

Score   / 7

Answer all parts of the questions. Show your workings (on a separate sheet of paper if necessary) and include the correct units in your answers.

1 a) Solve these simultaneous equations.

$y = x + 4$ and $y = x^2 - 2x$

U2 | U3

....

....

(5 marks)

b) Give a geometrical explanation of the result.

....

....

(2 marks)

2 The graph of $y = f(x)$ is sketched on the two grids below.

U3

a) Sketch the graph of $y = f(-x)$ on this grid.

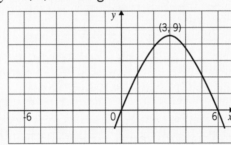

(2 marks)

b) Sketch the graph of $y = f(x + 2)$ on this grid.

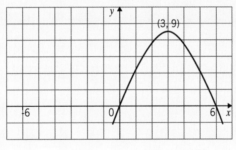

(2 marks)

3 The curve with equation $y = f(x)$ is translated so that the point at (0, 0) is mapped onto the point (-6, 0). Find the equation of the translated curve.

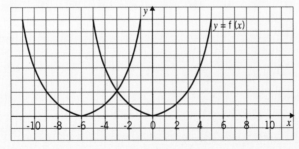

(2 marks)

Score   / 13

How well did you do?

| 0–5 Try again | 6–11 Getting there | 12–18 Good work | 19–24 Excellent! |

For more information on this topic, see pages 68–69 of your Success Revision Guide.

Algebra

55

Interpreting graphs

Multiple-choice questions

Choose just one answer, a, b, c or d. Circle your choice.

Use the graph opposite for these questions.
The graph represents Mrs Morgan's car journey.

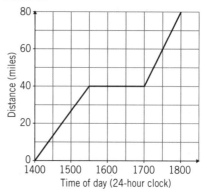

(U2)

1 At what speed did Mrs Morgan travel for the first hour and a half?

   a) 25mph   **b)** 28mph   **c)** 30mph   **d)** 26.7mph   (1 mark)

2 At what time did Mrs Morgan take a break from her car journey?

   a) 1530   **b)** 1600   **c)** 1400   **d)** 1500   (1 mark)

3 At what speed did Mrs Morgan travel between 1700 and 1800 hours?

   a) 60mph   **b)** 80mph   **c)** 35mph   **d)** 40mph   (1 mark)

Score   / 3

Short-answer questions

Answer all parts of each question.

1 Water is poured into these odd-shaped vases at a constant rate. Match each vase to the correct graph.

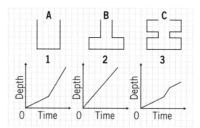

Vase A matches graph ....

Vase B matches graph ....

Vase C matches graph ....

(U2 U3)

(3 marks)

2 This is the graph of $y = x^2 - x - 6$

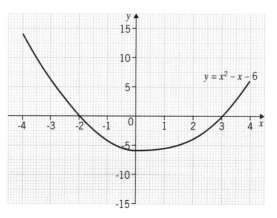

(U3)

  a) Use the graph to find the roots of the equation $x^2 - x - 6 = 0$

     .... and .... (2 marks)

  b) By drawing suitable straight lines on the graph, solve these equations:

    i) $x^2 - x - 6 = 2$ ....

    ii) $x^2 - 7 = 0$ .... (3 marks)

Score   / 8

Answer all parts of the questions. Show your workings (on a separate sheet of paper if necessary) and include the correct units in your answers.

1 U3

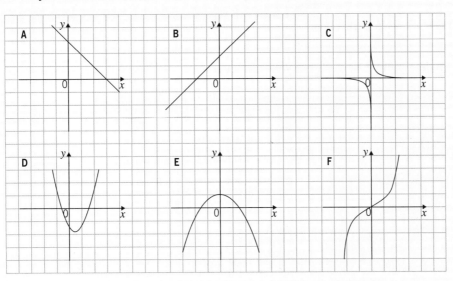

Each of the equations in the table represents one of the graphs A–F.
Complete the table by writing the correct letter of each graph in the correct place.

Equation	Graph
$y = x^2 - x - 6$	
$y = 6 - x^2$	
$y = x^3$	
$y = 3x + 2$	
$y = 5 - x$	
$y = \frac{2}{x}$	

(3 marks)

2 The sketch graph shows a curve $y = ab^x$ where $b > 0$.

The curve passes through the points (1, 6) and (3, 54).
Calculate the values of a and b.

$a = $ ....

$b = $ ....

(3 marks)

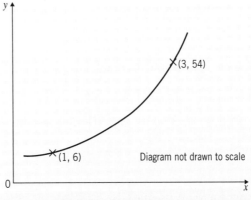

(3, 54)

(1, 6)   Diagram not drawn to scale

Score   / 6

How well did you do?

| 0–3 | Try again | 4–8 | Getting there | 9–13 | Good work | 14–17 | Excellent! |

For more information on this topic, see pages 70–71 of your Success Revision Guide.

57

Algebra

Measures & measurement

Multiple-choice questions

Choose just one answer, a, b, c or d. Circle your choice.

1 Jessica is 165cm tall to the nearest cm. What is the lower limit of her height?

   a) 164.5cm   **b)** 165.5cm   **c)** 165cm   **d)** 164.9cm

U1 U3

(1 mark)

2 Approximately how many pounds are in 4kg?

   a) 6.9   **b)** 12.4   **c)** 7.7   **d)** 8.8

U3

(1 mark)

3 What is 2500g in kilograms?

   a) 25kg   **b)** 2.5kg   **c)** 0.25kg   **d)** 250kg

(1 mark)

4 What is the volume of a piece of wood with density 680kg/m^{-3} and a mass 34kg? 🖩

   a) 0.5m^3 **b)** 20m^3 **c)** 2m^3 **d)** 0.05m^3

(1 mark)

5 A car travels for two and a half hours at a speed of 42mph. How far does the car travel? 🖩

   a) 96 miles   **b)** 100 miles   **c)** 105 miles   **d)** 140 miles

(1 mark)

Score   / 5

Short-answer questions

Answer all parts of each question.

1 Complete the statements below.

U3

   a) 8km = _____ m   **b)** 3250g = _____ kg

   c) 7 tonnes = _____ kg   **d)** 52cm = _____ m

   e) 2.7 litres = _____ ml   **f)** 262cm = _____ km

(6 marks)

2 Two towns are approximately 20km apart. Approximately how many miles is this? 🖩

(1 mark)

3 A recipe uses 600g of flour. Approximately how many pounds is this? 🖩

(1 mark)

4 Giovanni drove 200 miles in 3 hours and 20 minutes. At what average speed did he travel? 🖩

(2 marks)

5 What is the density of a toy if its mass is 200g and its volume is 2000cm^3?

(2 marks)

Score   / 12

GCSE-style questions

Answer all parts of the questions. Show your workings (on a separate sheet of paper if necessary) and include the correct units in your answers.

1 The length of the rectangle is 12.1cm to the nearest mm. The width of the rectangle is 6cm to the nearest cm. Write down the lower limits for the length and width of the rectangle.

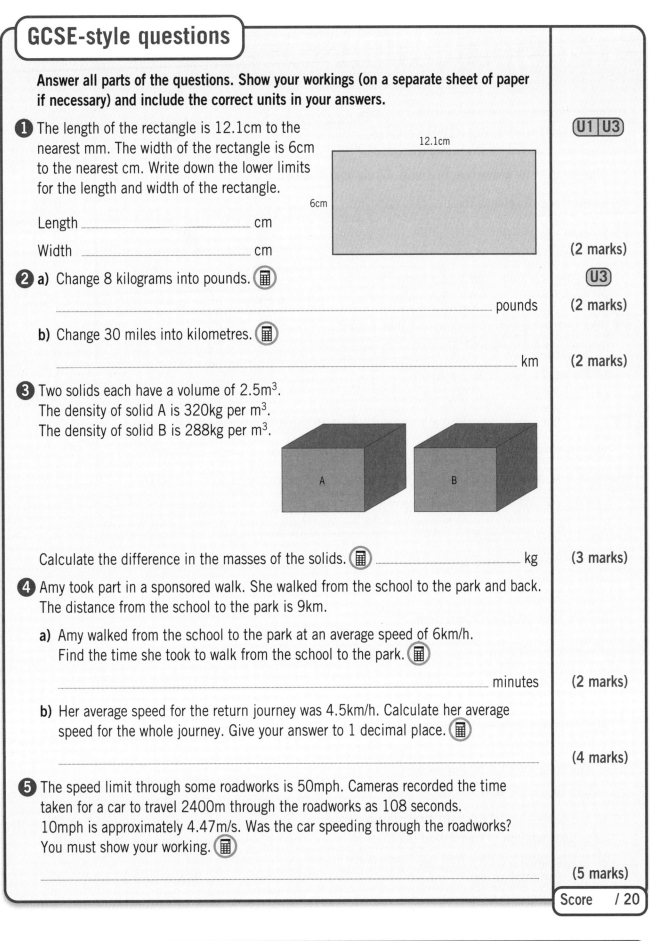

12.1cm

6cm

U1 U3

Length .... cm

Width .... cm   (2 marks)

2 **a)** Change 8 kilograms into pounds. 🔲

U3

.... pounds   (2 marks)

b) Change 30 miles into kilometres. 🔲

.... km   (2 marks)

3 Two solids each have a volume of 2.5m³.
The density of solid A is 320kg per m³.
The density of solid B is 288kg per m³.

A   B

Calculate the difference in the masses of the solids. 🔲 .... kg   (3 marks)

4 Amy took part in a sponsored walk. She walked from the school to the park and back. The distance from the school to the park is 9km.

a) Amy walked from the school to the park at an average speed of 6km/h. Find the time she took to walk from the school to the park. 🔲

.... minutes   (2 marks)

b) Her average speed for the return journey was 4.5km/h. Calculate her average speed for the whole journey. Give your answer to 1 decimal place. 🔲

.... (4 marks)

5 The speed limit through some roadworks is 50mph. Cameras recorded the time taken for a car to travel 2400m through the roadworks as 108 seconds. 10mph is approximately 4.47m/s. Was the car speeding through the roadworks? You must show your working. 🔲

.... (5 marks)

Score   / 20

Geometry and measures

How well did you do?

| 0–13 | Try again | 14–21 | Getting there | 22–29 | Good work | 30–37 | Excellent! |

For more information on this topic, see pages 76–77 of your Success Revision Guide.

Transformations 1

Multiple-choice questions

Choose just one answer, a, b, c or d. Circle your choice.

Questions 1–4 refer to the diagram opposite.

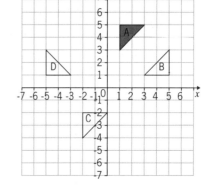

(U3)

1 What is the type of transformation that would map shape A onto shape B?

  a) Reflection   **b)** Scale factor
  c) Translation   **d)** Enlargement

(1 mark)

2 What is the type of transformation that would map shape A onto shape C?

  a) Reflection   **b)** Rotation
  c) Translation   **d)** Enlargement

(1 mark)

3 What is the type of transformation that would map shape A onto shape D?

  a) Reflection   **b)** Rotation   **c)** Translation   **d)** Enlargement

(1 mark)

4 What special name is given to the relationship between triangles A, B, C and D?

  a) Enlargement   **b)** Congruent   **c)** Translation   **d)** Similar

(1 mark)

Score   / 4

Short-answer questions

Answer all parts of each question.

1 On the grid, carry out the following transformations.

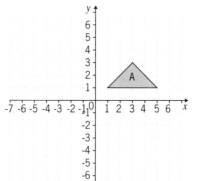

(U3)

  a) Reflect shape A in the *y*-axis.
     Call the new shape R.

(1 mark)

  b) Rotate shape A 90° clockwise, about (0, 0).
     Call the new shape S.

(1 mark)

  c) Translate shape A by the vector $\binom{-3}{4}$.
     Call the new shape T.

(1 mark)

2 All the shapes in the diagram are either a **reflection**, **rotation** or **translation** of object P. State the transformation that has taken place in each of the following.

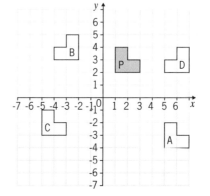

  a) P is transformed to A ....

(1 mark)

  b) P is transformed to B ....

(1 mark)

  c) P is transformed to C ....

(1 mark)

  d) P is transformed to D ....

(1 mark)

Score   / 7

GCSE-style questions

Answer all parts of the questions. Show your workings (on a separate sheet of paper if necessary) and include the correct units in your answers.

1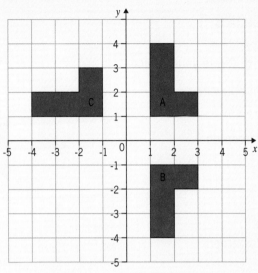

(U3)

a) Describe fully the single transformation that takes shape A onto shape B.

....

.... **(2 marks)**

b) Describe fully the single transformation that takes shape A onto shape C.

....

.... **(3 marks)**

2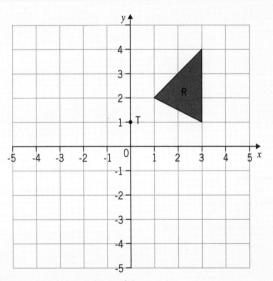

The triangle R has been drawn on the grid.

a) Rotate triangle R 90° clockwise about the point T (0, 1) and call the image P. **(3 marks)**

b) Translate triangle R by the vector $\binom{-4}{-3}$ and call the image Q. **(3 marks)**

Score   / 11

How well did you do?

| 0–6 | Try again | 7–10 | Getting there | 11–16 | Good work | 17–22 | Excellent! |

For more information on this topic, see pages 78–79 of your Success Revision Guide.

Transformations 2

Multiple-choice questions

Choose just one answer, a, b, c or d. Circle your choice.

Questions 1–3 refer to the diagram opposite.

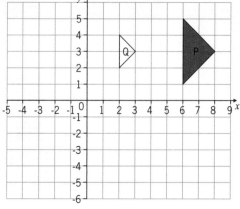

(U3)

1 Shape P is enlarged to give shape Q.
What is the scale factor of the enlargement?

   a) $\frac{1}{3}$ **b)** 2

   c) 3   **d)** $\frac{1}{2}$

(1 mark)

2 Shape Q is enlarged to give shape P.
What is the scale factor of the enlargement?

   a) $\frac{1}{3}$ **b)** 2

   c) 3   **d)** $\frac{1}{2}$

(1 mark)

3 What are the coordinates of the centre of the enlargement in both cases?

   a) (3, -2)   **b)** (-2, 3)   **c)** (-3, 4)   **d)** (0, 0)

(1 mark)

Score   / 3

Short-answer questions

Answer all parts of each question.

1 The diagram shows the position of three shapes, A, B and C.

  a) Describe the transformation that maps A onto C.

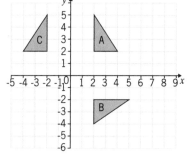

(U3)

(2 marks)

  b) Describe the transformation that maps A onto B.

                                                   (2 marks)

  c) Describe the transformation that maps B onto C.

(2 marks)

2 On the grid, enlarge
triangle PQR by a
scale factor of -2 with
centre of enlargement
(0, 0) and call the
image P'Q'R'.

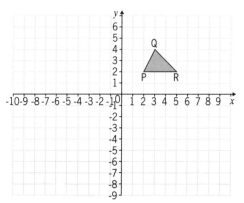

(3 marks)

Score   / 9

62

GCSE-style questions

Answer all parts of the questions. Show your workings (on a separate sheet of paper if necessary) and include the correct units in your answers.

1 Enlarge triangle N by a scale factor $\frac{1}{3}$ with centre R (-6, 7). (U3)

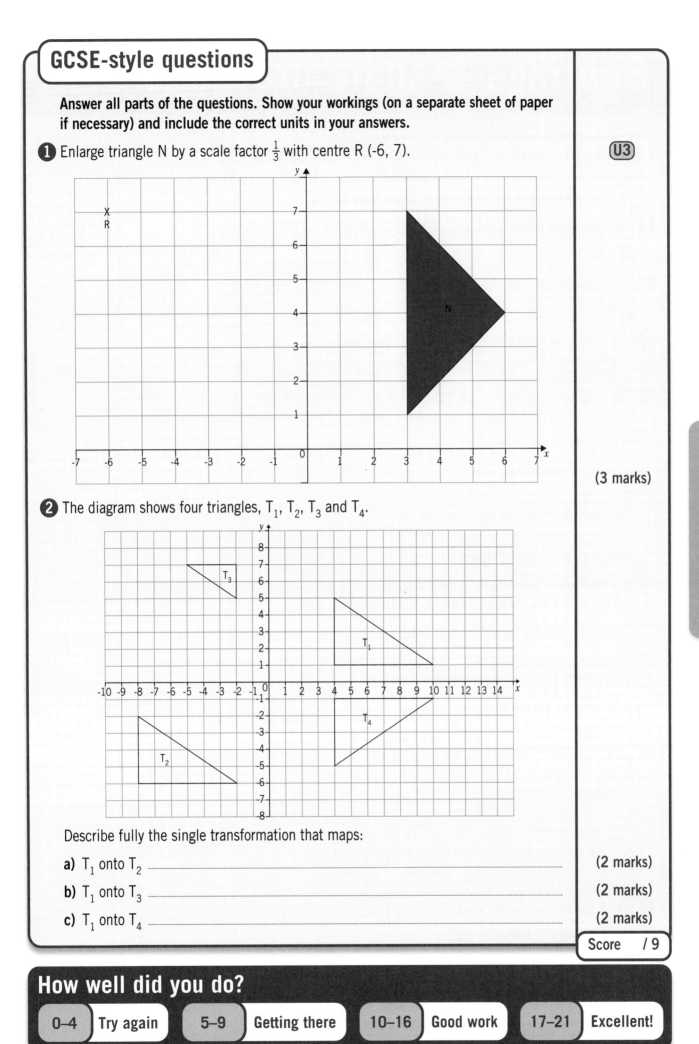

(3 marks)

2 The diagram shows four triangles, T_1, T_2, T_3 and T_4.

Describe fully the single transformation that maps:

a) T_1 onto T_2 .... (2 marks)

b) T_1 onto T_3 .... (2 marks)

c) T_1 onto T_4 .... (2 marks)

Score   / 9

How well did you do?

| 0–4 | Try again | 5–9 | Getting there | 10–16 | Good work | 17–21 | Excellent! |

For more information on this topic, see pages 80–81 of your Success Revision Guide.

Bearings & scale drawings

Multiple-choice questions

Choose just one answer, a, b, c or d. Circle your choice.

1 The bearing of P from Q is 050°. What is the bearing of Q from P?

   a) 130°   **b)** 50°   **c)** 230°   **d)** 310°

(U3)

(1 mark)

2 The bearing of R from S is 130°. What is the bearing of S from R?

   a) 310°   **b)** 230°   **c)** 050°   **d)** 200°

(1 mark)

3 The bearing of A from B is 240°. What is the bearing of B from A?

   a) 120°   **b)** 60°   **c)** 320°   **d)** 060°

(1 mark)

4 The length of a car park is 25 metres. A scale diagram of the car park is being drawn to a scale of 1cm to 5 metres. What is the length of the car park on the scale diagram?

   a) 500mm   **b)** 5cm   **c)** 50cm   **d)** 5m

(1 mark)

Score   / 4

Short-answer questions

Answer all parts of each question.

1 The scale on a road map is 1 : 50 000. Two towns are 20cm apart on the map. Work out the real distance, in km, between the two towns.

_____ km

(U3)

(2 marks)

2 A ship sails on a bearing of 065° for 10km. It then continues on a bearing of 120° for a further 15km to a port (P).

a) On a separate piece of paper, draw, using a scale of 1cm to 2km, an accurate scale drawing of this information.

(3 marks)

b) Measure on your diagram the direct distance between the starting point and port P.

_____ km

(1 mark)

c) What is the bearing of port P from the starting point?

_____ °

(1 mark)

3 Is this statement true or false?

'The bearing of B from A is 060°.'

_____

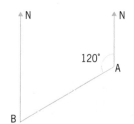

(1 mark)

Score   / 8

GCSE-style questions

Answer all parts of the questions. Show your workings (on a separate sheet of paper if necessary) and include the correct units in your answers.

1 The diagram shows a scale drawing of one side AB of a triangular playground, ABC.

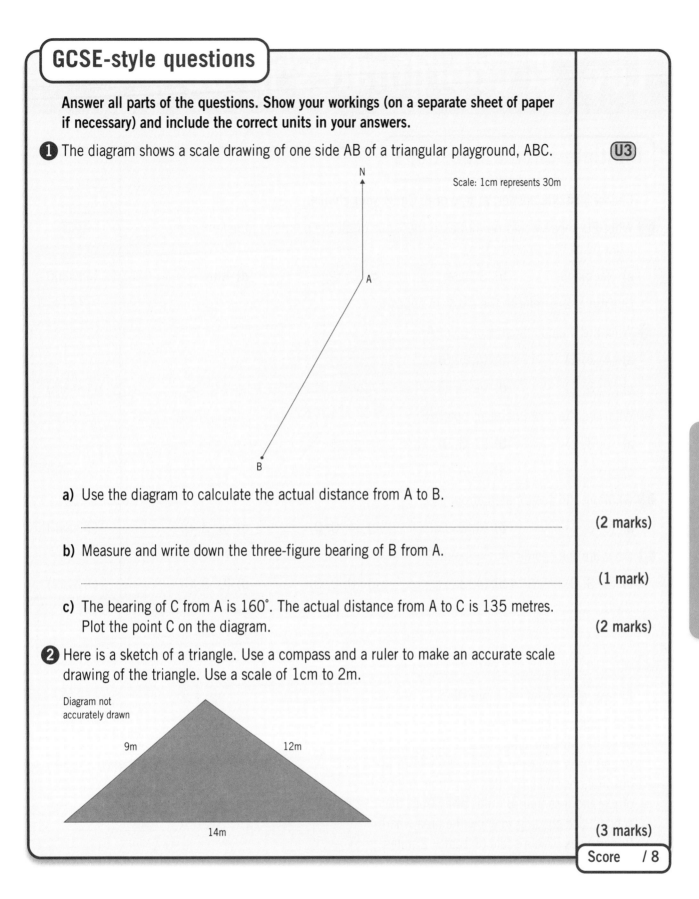

N

Scale: 1cm represents 30m

A

B

U3

a) Use the diagram to calculate the actual distance from A to B.

_____ (2 marks)

b) Measure and write down the three-figure bearing of B from A.

_____ (1 mark)

c) The bearing of C from A is 160°. The actual distance from A to C is 135 metres. Plot the point C on the diagram. (2 marks)

2 Here is a sketch of a triangle. Use a compass and a ruler to make an accurate scale drawing of the triangle. Use a scale of 1cm to 2m.

Diagram not accurately drawn

9m

12m

14m

(3 marks)

Score   / 8

How well did you do?

| 0–4 | Try again | 5–10 | Getting there | 11–15 | Good work | 16–20 | Excellent! |

For more information on this topic, see pages 84–85 of your Success Revision Guide.

65

Loci & coordinates in 3D

Multiple-choice questions

Choose just one answer, a, b, c or d. Circle your choice.

1 What 2D shape would be formed if the locus of all the points equidistant from a fixed point P is drawn?

a) Rectangle　　　**b)** Square　　　**c)** Circle　　　**d)** Kite

 U3

(1 mark)

Questions 2–5 refer to the diagram opposite.

2 What are the coordinates of point A?

a) (4, 3, 1)　　　**b)** (4, 3, 0)

c) (0, 3, 1)　　　**d)** (4, 0, 1)

(1 mark)

3 What are the coordinates of point B?

a) (0, 3, 1)　　　**b)** (0, 0, 0)

c) (4, 3, 0)　　　**d)** (0, 3, 0)

(1 mark)

4 What are the coordinates of point C?

a) (0, 3, 1)　　**b)** (4, 3, 1)　　**c)** (4, 0, 0)　　**d)** (4, 3, 0)

(1 mark)

5 What are the coordinates of point D?

a) (4, 3, 0)　　**b)** (4, 3, 1)　　**c)** (0, 0, 0)　　**d)** (0, 3, 0)

(1 mark)

Score　　/ 5

Short-answer questions

Answer all parts of each question.

1 The diagram shows the position of the post office (P), the hospital (H) and the school (S). Robert lives less than 4 miles away from the hospital, less than 5 miles away from the post office and less than 8 miles away from the school. Use shading to show the area where Robert lives. Use a scale of 1cm = 2 miles.

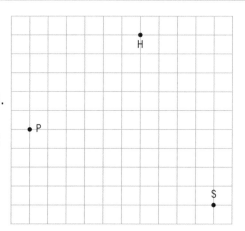

U3

(4 marks)

2 The diagram shows a solid. Complete the coordinates for each of the vertices listed below.

R = (.........., ..., ...)

S = (.........., ..., ...)

T = (.........., ..., ...)

U = (.........., ..., ...)

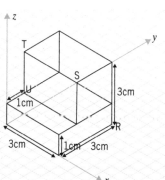

(4 marks)

Score　　/ 8

GCSE-style questions

Answer all parts of the questions. Show your workings (on a separate sheet of paper if necessary) and include the correct units in your answers.

1 In this question you should use a ruler and a compass only for the constructions. (U3)

Triangle ABC is the plan of an adventure playground, drawn to a scale of 1cm to 20m.

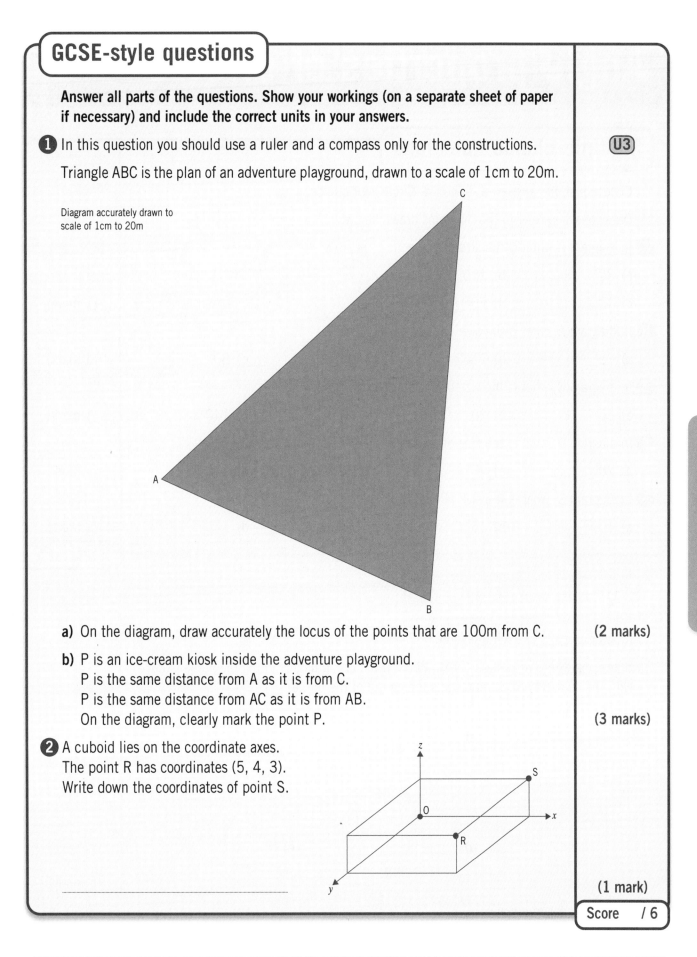

Diagram accurately drawn to scale of 1cm to 20m

a) On the diagram, draw accurately the locus of the points that are 100m from C. (2 marks)

b) P is an ice-cream kiosk inside the adventure playground.
P is the same distance from A as it is from C.
P is the same distance from AC as it is from AB.
On the diagram, clearly mark the point P. (3 marks)

2 A cuboid lies on the coordinate axes.
The point R has coordinates (5, 4, 3).
Write down the coordinates of point S.

(1 mark)

Score   / 6

For more information on this topic, see page 88 of your Success Revision Guide.

Angle properties of circles

Multiple-choice questions

Choose just one answer, a, b, c or d. Circle your choice.

Questions 1–5 refer to the diagrams drawn below.

U3

1 In diagram A, what is the size of angle *a*?

a) 80°   b) 110°

c) 100°   d) 70°

(1 mark)

Diagram A   Diagram B   Diagram C

2 In diagram A, what is the size of angle *b*?

a) 70°   b) 110°   c) 100°   d) 80°

(1 mark)

3 In diagram B, what is the size of angle *c*?

a) 35°   b) 70°   c) 100°   d) 140°

(1 mark)

4 In diagram B, what is the size of angle *d*?

a) 70°   b) 35°   c) 100°   d) 140°

(1 mark)

5 In diagram C, what is the size of angle *e*?

a) 100°   b) 45°   c) 90°   d) 110°

(1 mark)

Score   / 5

Short-answer questions

Answer all parts of each question.

1 Some angles are written on cards. Match the missing angles in the diagrams below with the correct card. O represents the centre of the circle.

U3

50° 60° 82° 65° 18°

a)

b)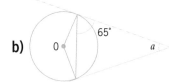

c)

d)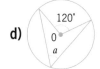

e)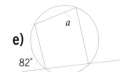

(5 marks)

2 John says, 'Angle *a* is 42°.'

Explain whether John is correct.

(1 mark)

Score   / 6

Answer all parts of the questions. Show your workings (on a separate sheet of paper if necessary) and include the correct units in your answers.

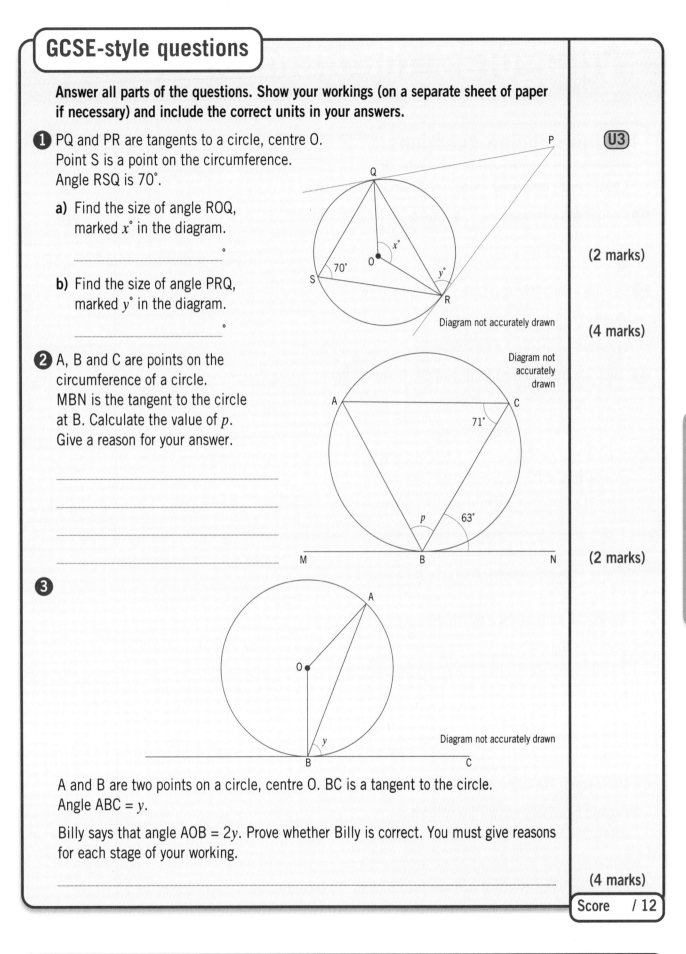

1 PQ and PR are tangents to a circle, centre O.
Point S is a point on the circumference.
Angle RSQ is 70°.

    a) Find the size of angle ROQ,
    marked $x°$ in the diagram.

    _____ °

    (2 marks)

    b) Find the size of angle PRQ,
    marked $y°$ in the diagram.

    _____ °

    (4 marks)

2 A, B and C are points on the
circumference of a circle.
MBN is the tangent to the circle
at B. Calculate the value of p.
Give a reason for your answer.

_____

_____

_____

_____

(2 marks)

3

A and B are two points on a circle, centre O. BC is a tangent to the circle.
Angle ABC = y.

Billy says that angle AOB = $2y$. Prove whether Billy is correct. You must give reasons
for each stage of your working.

_____

(4 marks)

Score   / 12

U3

Geometry and measures

How well did you do?

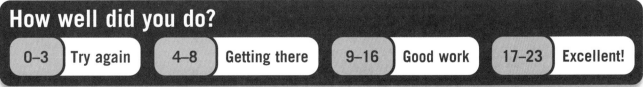

| 0–3 | Try again | 4–8 | Getting there | 9–16 | Good work | 17–23 | Excellent! |

For more information on this topic, see page 89 of your Success Revision Guide.

69

Pythagoras' theorem

Multiple-choice questions

Choose just one answer, a, b, c or d. Circle your choice.

1 Point C has coordinates (-3, 5) and point D has coordinates (5, 12). What are the coordinates of the midpoint of the line CD?

 U3

   a) (1, 3.5)   **b)** (4, 8.5)   **c)** (4, 3.5)   **d)** (1, 8.5)   **(1 mark)**

2 Calculate the missing length y of this triangle.

   a) 169cm   **b)** 13cm

   c) 17cm   **d)** 84.5cm   **(1 mark)**

12cm y 5cm

3 Calculate the missing length y of this triangle.

   a) 13.2cm   **b)** 5cm

   c) 25cm   **d)** 625cm   **(1 mark)**

20cm y 15cm

4 Point A has coordinates (1, 4) and point B has coordinates (4, 10). What are the coordinates of the midpoint of the line AB?

   a) (5, 14)   **b)** (3, 6)   **c)** (2.5, 7)   **d)** (1.5, 3)   **(1 mark)**

Score   / 4

Short-answer questions

Answer all parts of each question.

1 Calculate the missing lengths of these right-angled triangles. Give your answer to 3 significant figures, where appropriate.

U3

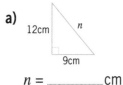

a) 12cm n 9cm   **b)** n 15.2cm 8.5cm   **c)** n 22.1cm 19cm   **d)** 31cm n 18.9cm

   $n =$ .... cm $n =$ .... cm $n =$ .... cm $n =$ .... cm   **(8 marks)**

2 Molly says, 'The angle $x°$ in this triangle is 90°.'

Explain how Molly knows this without measuring the size of the angle.

12cm   13cm $x°$ 5cm

....   **(2 marks)**

3 Colin says, 'The length of this line is $\sqrt{45}$ units. The coordinates of the midpoint are (3.5, 8).'

Decide whether these statements are true or false. Give an explanation for your answer.

   (5, 11)   (2, 5)

....
....   **(2 marks)**

Score   / 12

Answer all parts of the questions. Show your workings (on a separate sheet of paper if necessary) and include the correct units in your answers.

❶ Calculate the perpendicular height of this isosceles triangle. Give your answer to 1 decimal place.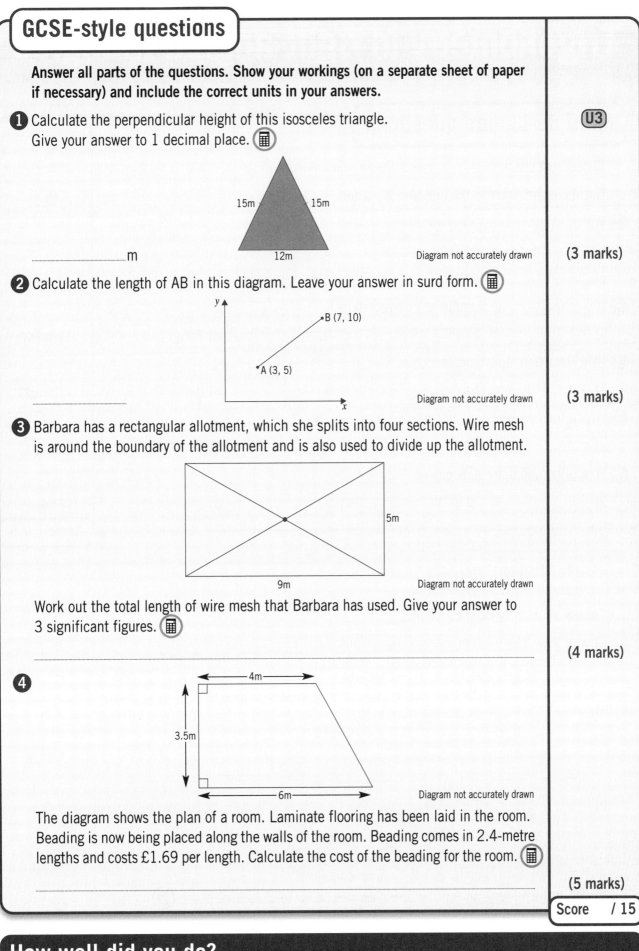

(U3)

............................m

15m   15m

12m   Diagram not accurately drawn

(3 marks)

❷ Calculate the length of AB in this diagram. Leave your answer in surd form.

y

•B (7, 10)

•A (3, 5)

x

....

Diagram not accurately drawn

(3 marks)

❸ Barbara has a rectangular allotment, which she splits into four sections. Wire mesh is around the boundary of the allotment and is also used to divide up the allotment.

5m

9m   Diagram not accurately drawn

Work out the total length of wire mesh that Barbara has used. Give your answer to 3 significant figures.

(4 marks)

❹

4m

3.5m

6m   Diagram not accurately drawn

The diagram shows the plan of a room. Laminate flooring has been laid in the room. Beading is now being placed along the walls of the room. Beading comes in 2.4-metre lengths and costs £1.69 per length. Calculate the cost of the beading for the room.

(5 marks)

Score   / 15

How well did you do?

0–7 Try again   8–14 Getting there   15–23 Good work   24–31 Excellent!

For more information on this topic, see pages 90–91 of your Success Revision Guide.

Geometry and measures

Trigonometry in right-angled triangles

Multiple-choice questions

Choose just one answer, a, b, c or d. Circle your choice.

Questions 1–5 refer to the diagram opposite.

1 Which length is opposite angle x?

a) PQ   **b)** PR

c) QR   **d)** RX

(1 mark)

2 Which length of the triangle is the hypotenuse?

a) PQ   **b)** PR   **c)** QR   **d)** RX

(1 mark)

3 Which fraction represents tan x?

a) $\frac{3}{5}$ **b)** $\frac{4}{3}$ **c)** $\frac{4}{5}$ **d)** $\frac{3}{4}$

(1 mark)

4 Which fraction represents sin x?

a) $\frac{3}{5}$ **b)** $\frac{4}{3}$ **c)** $\frac{5}{3}$ **d)** $\frac{4}{5}$

(1 mark)

5 Which fraction represents cos x?

a) $\frac{3}{5}$ **b)** $\frac{3}{4}$ **c)** $\frac{4}{5}$ **d)** $\frac{5}{4}$

(1 mark)

Score   / 5

Short-answer questions

Answer all parts of each question.

1 Choose a card for each of the missing lengths, n, on the triangles. The lengths have been rounded to 1 decimal place.

6.3 cm   6.7 cm   13.8 cm   5 cm   14.9 cm

a)

$n =$ _____ cm

b)

$n =$ _____ cm

c)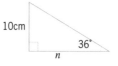

$n =$ _____ cm

d)

$n =$ _____ cm

e)

$n =$ _____ cm

(5 marks)

2 Work out the missing angle, x, in the diagrams below to 1 decimal place.

a)

$x =$ _____ °

b)

$x =$ _____ °

c)

$x =$ _____ °

(6 marks)

Score   / 11

Answer all parts of the questions. Show your workings (on a separate sheet of paper if necessary) and include the correct units in your answers.

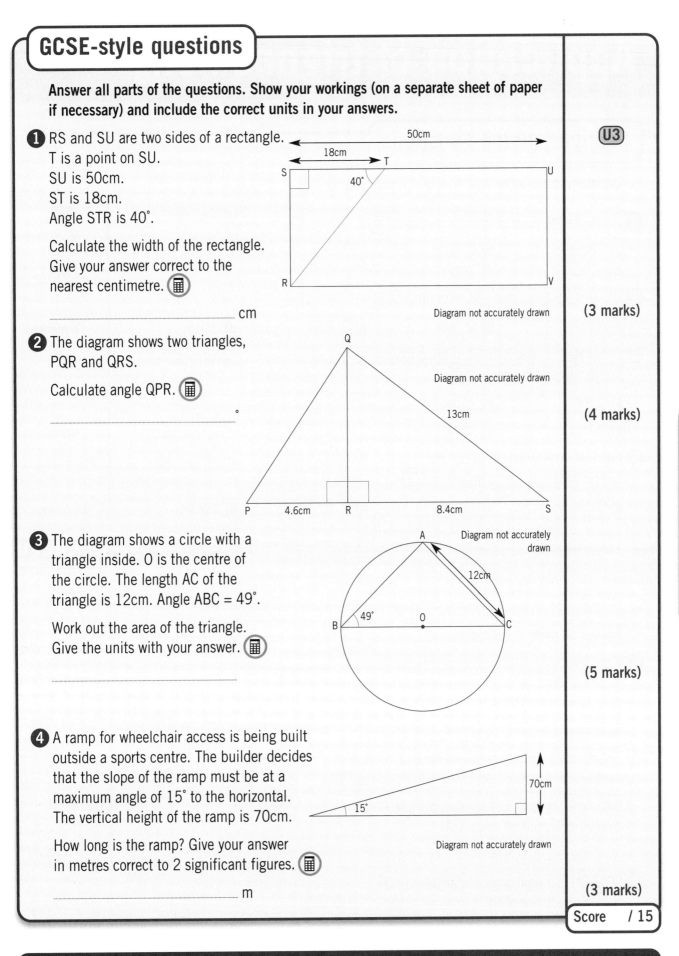

1 RS and SU are two sides of a rectangle.
T is a point on SU.
SU is 50cm.
ST is 18cm.
Angle STR is 40°.

Calculate the width of the rectangle. Give your answer correct to the nearest centimetre. 🖩

_____ cm

Diagram not accurately drawn

(3 marks)

(U3)

2 The diagram shows two triangles, PQR and QRS.

Calculate angle QPR. 🖩

Diagram not accurately drawn

_____ °

(4 marks)

3 The diagram shows a circle with a triangle inside. O is the centre of the circle. The length AC of the triangle is 12cm. Angle ABC = 49°.

Work out the area of the triangle. Give the units with your answer. 🖩

Diagram not accurately drawn

_____

(5 marks)

4 A ramp for wheelchair access is being built outside a sports centre. The builder decides that the slope of the ramp must be at a maximum angle of 15° to the horizontal. The vertical height of the ramp is 70cm.

How long is the ramp? Give your answer in metres correct to 2 significant figures. 🖩

Diagram not accurately drawn

_____ m

(3 marks)

Score   / 15

Geometry and measures

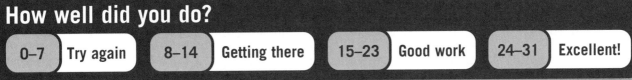
For more information on this topic, see pages 92–93 of your Success Revision Guide.

Application of trigonometry

Multiple-choice questions

Choose just one answer, a, b, c or d. Circle your choice.

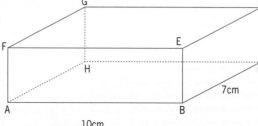

1 Calculate the value of x in the triangle. 📱

Diagram not accurately drawn

U3

   a) 13cm   **b)** 8.7cm

   c) 7.5cm   **d)** 10cm

(1 mark)

2 Calculate the value of y in the triangle. 📱

   a) 13cm   **b)** 8.7cm   **c)** 7.5cm   **d)** 10cm

(1 mark)

3 Calculate the length of AC in the cuboid to the nearest centimetre. 📱

Diagram not accurately drawn

   a) 13cm   **b)** 11cm

   c) 12cm   **d)** 14cm

(1 mark)

4 Calculate the length of AD in the cuboid to the nearest centimetre. 📱

   a) 11cm   **b)** 13cm   **c)** 12cm   **d)** 14cm

(1 mark)

Score   / 4

Short-answer questions

Answer all parts of each question.

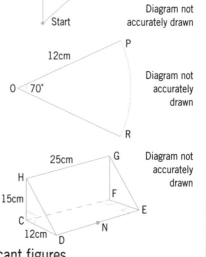

1 A ship sails 20km due north and then 50km due east. What is the bearing of the finishing point from the starting point? 📱

U3

Bearing = _____ °

(2 marks)

2 The diagram represents the sector of a circle with centre O and radius 12cm. Angle POR equals 70°.

Calculate the length of the straight line PR, correct to 1 decimal place. 📱

_____ cm

(3 marks)

3 CDEFGH is a right-angled triangular prism. N is the midpoint of DE.

Diagram not accurately drawn

   a) Are the following statements true or false?

     i) The length HD is 19.2cm, correct to 3 significant figures. _____

(1 mark)

     ii) The size of angle HDC is 51.3°, correct to 1 decimal place. _____

(1 mark)

   b) Calculate the size of angle HNC, correct to 1 decimal place. 📱 _____ °

(3 marks)

Score   / 10

GCSE-style questions

Answer all parts of the questions. Show your workings (on a separate sheet of paper if necessary) and include the correct units in your answers.

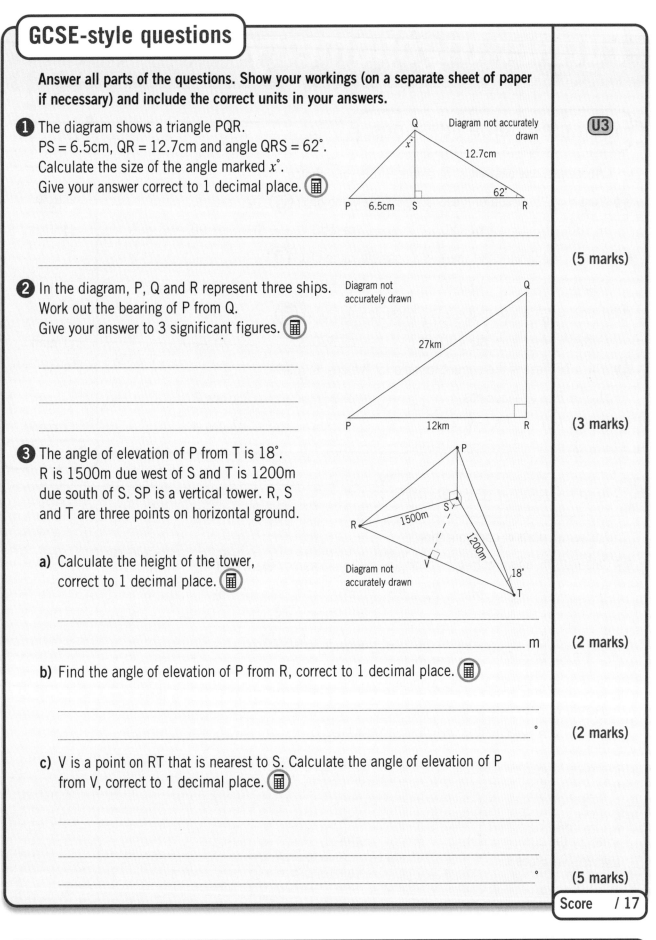

1 The diagram shows a triangle PQR.
PS = 6.5cm, QR = 12.7cm and angle QRS = 62°.
Calculate the size of the angle marked $x°$.
Give your answer correct to 1 decimal place. 🔢

(U3)

Q Diagram not accurately drawn
$x°$
12.7cm
62°
P   6.5cm   S   R

(5 marks)

2 In the diagram, P, Q and R represent three ships.
Work out the bearing of P from Q.
Give your answer to 3 significant figures. 🔢

Diagram not accurately drawn

Q
27km
P   12km   R

(3 marks)

3 The angle of elevation of P from T is 18°.
R is 1500m due west of S and T is 1200m
due south of S. SP is a vertical tower. R, S
and T are three points on horizontal ground.

P
S
R   1500m
1200m
V
18°
T
Diagram not accurately drawn

a) Calculate the height of the tower,
correct to 1 decimal place. 🔢

_____ m   (2 marks)

b) Find the angle of elevation of P from R, correct to 1 decimal place. 🔢

_____ °   (2 marks)

c) V is a point on RT that is nearest to S. Calculate the angle of elevation of P
from V, correct to 1 decimal place. 🔢

_____ °   (5 marks)

Score   / 17

How well did you do?

0–10 Try again   11–17 Getting there   18–24 Good work   25–31 Excellent!

For more information on this topic, see pages 92–95 of your Success Revision Guide.

Further trigonometry

Multiple-choice questions

Choose just one answer, a, b, c or d. Circle your choice.

1 If sin x = 0.5, which of these is a possible value of x?

   a) 180°   **b)** 120°   **c)** 150°   **d)** 90°

(U3)

(1 mark)

2 If cos x = 0.5, which of these is a possible value of x?

   a) 300°   **b)** 150°   **c)** 65°   **d)** 120°

(1 mark)

3 If sin x = $\frac{\sqrt{3}}{2}$, which of these is a possible value of x?

   a) 320°   **b)** 400°   **c)** 360°   **d)** 420°

(1 mark)

4 Which of these is the correct formula for the cosine rule?

   a) $a^2 = b^2 - c^2 + 2bc \cos A$ **b)** $b^2 = a^2 + c^2 - 2bc \cos B$

   c) $a^2 = b^2 + c^2 - 2bc \cos A$ **d)** $c^2 = b^2 + a^2 - 2ab \cos A$

(1 mark)

Score   / 4

Short-answer questions

Answer all parts of each question.

1 Calculate the missing lengths or angles in the diagrams below.

Diagrams not accurately drawn

(U3)

a)   **b)**    **c)**   **d)**

   x = ... cm x = ... cm x = ... ° x = ... °

(8 marks)

2 Isobel says, 'The area of this triangle is 70cm².'

Decide, with working to justify your answer, whether this statement is correct or incorrect.

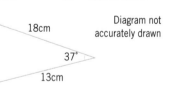

Diagram not accurately drawn

....

....

(2 marks)

3 The diagram shows a sketch of part of the curve y = f(x), where f(x) = cos x°.

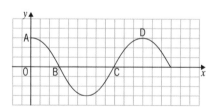

a) Write down the coordinates of the following points.

   A (............, ...)   B (............, ...)   C (............, ...)   D (............, ...)

(4 marks)

b) On the same diagram, sketch the graph of y = cos 2x.

(3 marks)

Score   / 17

Answer all parts of the questions. Show your workings (on a separate sheet of paper if necessary) and include the correct units in your answers.

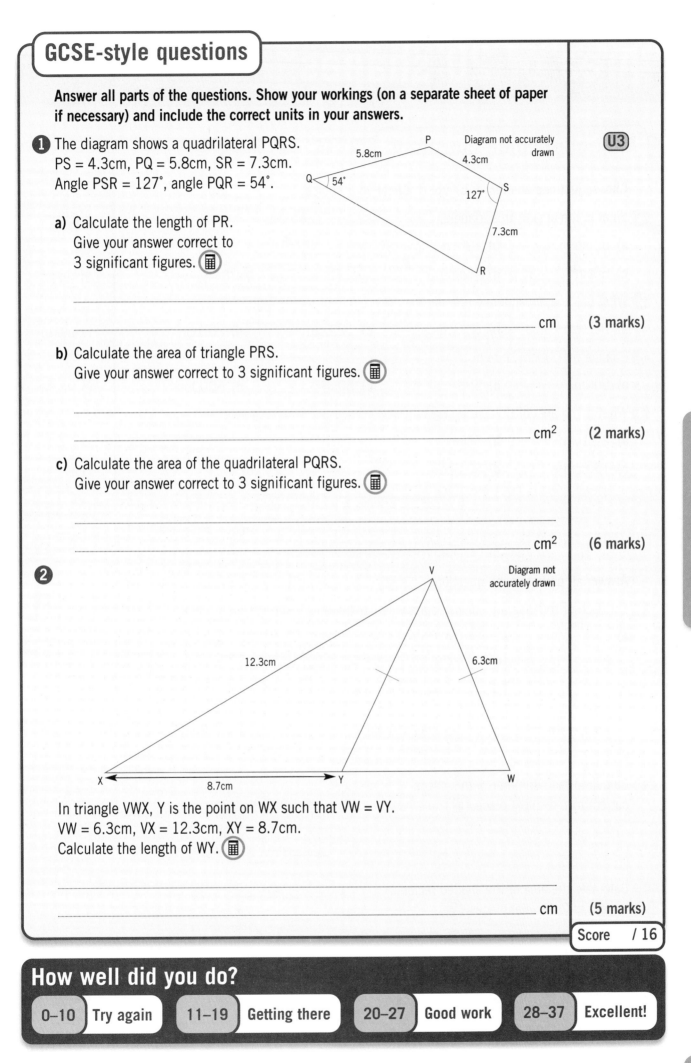

① The diagram shows a quadrilateral PQRS.
PS = 4.3cm, PQ = 5.8cm, SR = 7.3cm.
Angle PSR = 127°, angle PQR = 54°.

Diagram not accurately drawn

U3

a) Calculate the length of PR.
   Give your answer correct to
   3 significant figures. 🖩

   _____ cm   **(3 marks)**

b) Calculate the area of triangle PRS.
   Give your answer correct to 3 significant figures. 🖩

   _____ cm²   **(2 marks)**

c) Calculate the area of the quadrilateral PQRS.
   Give your answer correct to 3 significant figures. 🖩

   _____ cm²   **(6 marks)**

②

Diagram not accurately drawn

In triangle VWX, Y is the point on WX such that VW = VY.
VW = 6.3cm, VX = 12.3cm, XY = 8.7cm.
Calculate the length of WY. 🖩

_____ cm   **(5 marks)**

Score   / 16

Geometry and measures

How well did you do?

| 0–10 | Try again | 11–19 | Getting there | 20–27 | Good work | 28–37 | Excellent! |

For more information on this topic, see pages 96–97 of your Success Revision Guide.

Area of 2D shapes

Multiple-choice questions

Choose just one answer, a, b, c or d. Circle your choice.

1 What is the area of this triangle?

a) 60mm^2 b) 120cm^2

c) 60cm^2 d) 46cm^2

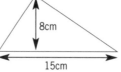

(U3)

(1 mark)

2 What is the approximate circumference of a circle of radius 4cm?

a) 25.1cm^2 b) 50.3cm   c) 12.6cm   d) 25.1cm

(1 mark)

3 Change 50 000cm^2 into m^2.

a) 500m^2 b) 5m^2 c) 50m^2 d) 5000m^2

(1 mark)

4 What is the area of this circle? 📟

a) 25.1cm^2 b) 55cm^2

c) 12.6cm^2 d) 50.3cm^2

(1 mark)

Score   / 4

Short-answer questions

Answer all parts of each question.

1 For each of the diagrams below, state whether the area given is true or false.

(U3)

a)

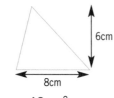

Area = 48cm^2

b)

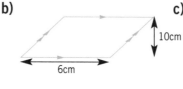

Area = 60cm^2

c)

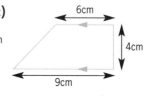

Area = 108cm^2

(3 marks)

2 Calculate the perimeter of this shape, correct to 1 decimal place. 📟

_____ cm

(3 marks)

3 Calculate the area of the shaded region, correct to 2 decimal places. 📟

_____ cm^2

(3 marks)

4 Change 7m^2 to cm^2. _____ cm^2

(2 marks)

Score   / 11

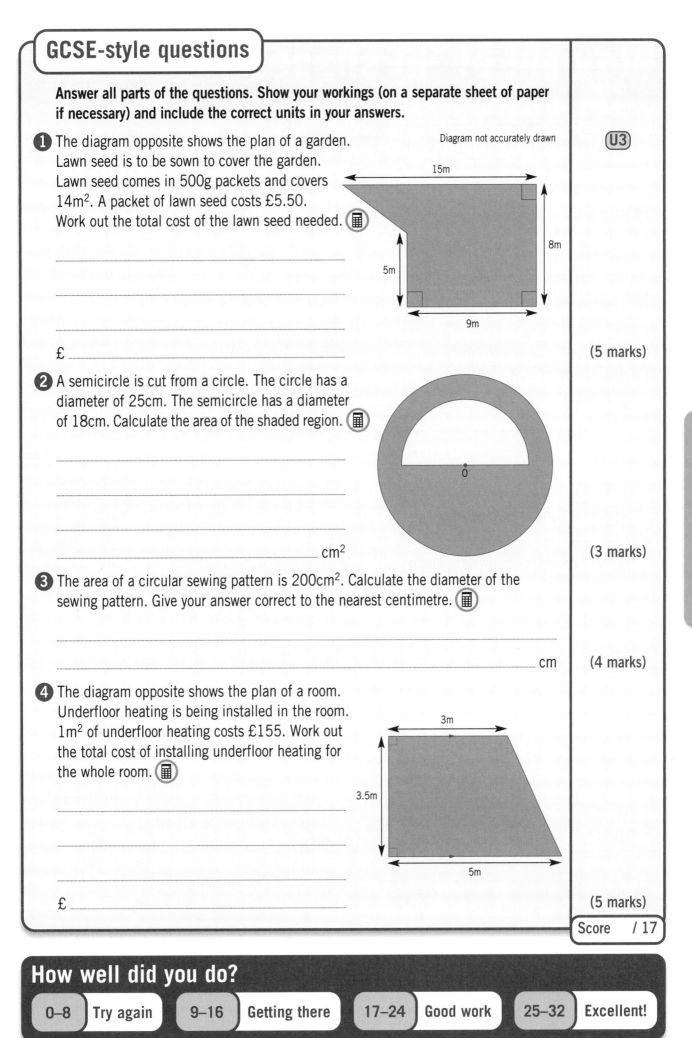

GCSE-style questions

Answer all parts of the questions. Show your workings (on a separate sheet of paper if necessary) and include the correct units in your answers.

1 The diagram opposite shows the plan of a garden. Lawn seed is to be sown to cover the garden. Lawn seed comes in 500g packets and covers 14m². A packet of lawn seed costs £5.50. Work out the total cost of the lawn seed needed. 🖩

Diagram not accurately drawn

U3

15m

8m

5m

9m

£ .... (5 marks)

2 A semicircle is cut from a circle. The circle has a diameter of 25cm. The semicircle has a diameter of 18cm. Calculate the area of the shaded region. 🖩

O

.... cm² (3 marks)

3 The area of a circular sewing pattern is 200cm². Calculate the diameter of the sewing pattern. Give your answer correct to the nearest centimetre. 🖩

.... cm (4 marks)

4 The diagram opposite shows the plan of a room. Underfloor heating is being installed in the room. 1m² of underfloor heating costs £155. Work out the total cost of installing underfloor heating for the whole room. 🖩

3m

3.5m

5m

£ .... (5 marks)

Score   / 17

Geometry and measures

How well did you do?

| 0–8 | Try again | 9–16 | Getting there | 17–24 | Good work | 25–32 | Excellent! |

For more information on this topic, see pages 98–99 of your Success Revision Guide.

Volume of 3D shapes

Multiple-choice questions

Choose just one answer, a, b, c or d. Circle your choice.

1 What is the volume of this prism?

a) 64cm³   b) 240cm³

c) 120cm³   d) 20cm³

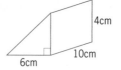

U3

(1 mark)

2 A cube of volume 2cm³ is enlarged by a scale factor of 3. What is the volume of the enlarged cube?

a) 6cm³   b) 27cm³   c) 54cm³   d) 18cm³

(1 mark)

3 What is 5m³ in cm³?

a) 500cm³   b) 5000cm³   c) 500 000cm³   d) 5 000 000cm³

(1 mark)

Score   / 3

Short-answer questions

Answer all parts of each question.

1 Emily says, 'The volume of this prism is 345.6m³.'
Is Emily correct? Show working out to justify your answer. 📱

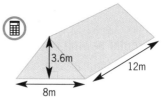

U3

_____

_____

(1 mark)

2 Calculate the volume of this cylinder, clearly stating your units. 📱

_____

_____

(2 marks)

3 If the volume of both solids is the same, work out the height of the cylinder to 1 decimal place. 📱

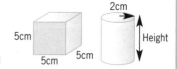

_____ cm

(4 marks)

4 The volume of a cube is 141cm³. Each length of the cube is enlarged by a scale factor of 3. What is the volume of the enlarged cube? 📱

_____ cm³

(2 marks)

5 Work out the surface area of the triangular prism. 📱

_____ cm²

(4 marks)

Score   / 13

GCSE-style questions

Answer all parts of the questions. Show your workings (on a separate sheet of paper if necessary) and include the correct units in your answers.

1 A cube has a surface area of 96cm². Work out the volume of the cube. 🖩 (U3)

_____

_____ cm³   **(4 marks)**

2 A metal door wedge is in the shape of a prism with cross-section VWXY. VW = 7cm, VY = 15cm, WX = 9cm. The width of the door wedge is 0.08m.

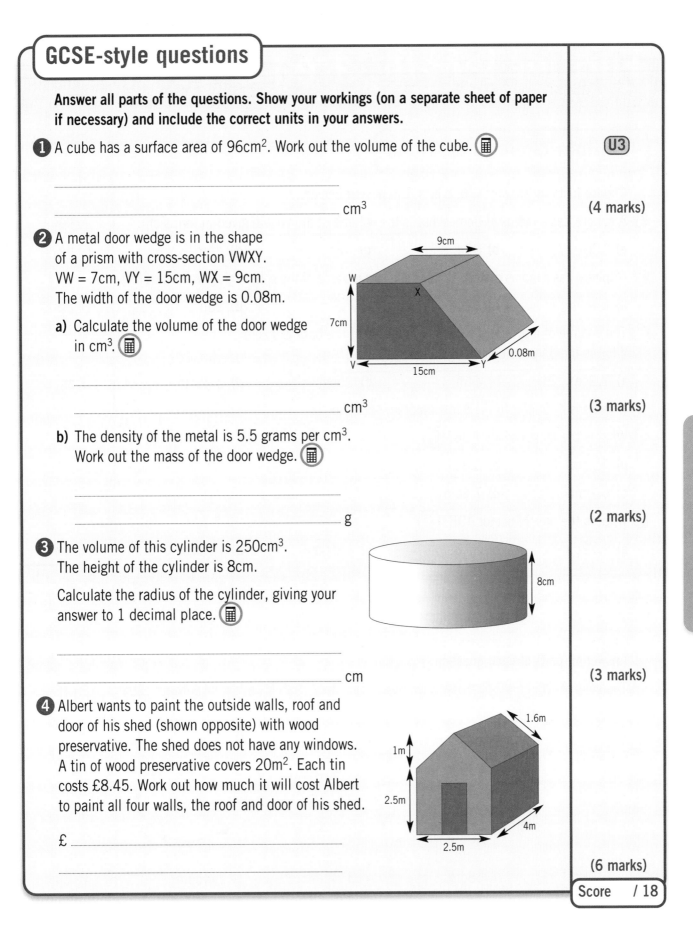

  a) Calculate the volume of the door wedge in cm³. 🖩

  _____

  _____ cm³   **(3 marks)**

  b) The density of the metal is 5.5 grams per cm³. Work out the mass of the door wedge. 🖩

  _____

  _____ g   **(2 marks)**

3 The volume of this cylinder is 250cm³. The height of the cylinder is 8cm.

Calculate the radius of the cylinder, giving your answer to 1 decimal place. 🖩

_____

_____ cm   **(3 marks)**

4 Albert wants to paint the outside walls, roof and door of his shed (shown opposite) with wood preservative. The shed does not have any windows. A tin of wood preservative covers 20m². Each tin costs £8.45. Work out how much it will cost Albert to paint all four walls, the roof and door of his shed.

£ _____

_____   **(6 marks)**

Score   / 18

Geometry and measures

How well did you do?

0–9 **Try again**   10–18 **Getting there**   19–26 **Good work**   27–34 **Excellent!**

For more information on this topic, see pages 100–101 of your Success Revision Guide.   **81**

Further length, area & volume

Geometry and measures

Multiple-choice questions

Choose just one answer, a, b, c or d. Circle your choice.

1 A sphere has a radius of 3cm. What is the volume of the sphere given in terms of π?

a) 12π   **b)** 36π   **c)** 42π   **d)** $\frac{81}{4}$π

(U3)

(1 mark)

2 A sphere has a radius of 4cm. What is the surface area of the sphere given in terms of π?

a) 64π   **b)** 32π   **c)** $\frac{256}{3}$π   **d)** 25π

(1 mark)

3 The volume of a pyramid is 25cm³. The area of the base is 12cm².
What is the perpendicular height of the pyramid?

a) 7.2cm   **b)** 4cm   **c)** 25cm   **d)** 6.25cm

(1 mark)

Questions 4–5 refer to the circle diagram opposite.

4 What is the length of arc AOB? 🔲

a) 5.2cm   **b)** 5.8cm

c) 6.2cm   **d)** 7.4cm

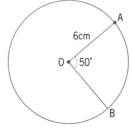

(1 mark)

5 What is the area of sector AOB? 🔲

a) 15.2cm²   **b)** 25.3cm²   **c)** 15.7cm²   **d)** 16.9cm²

(1 mark)

Score   / 5

Short-answer questions

Answer all parts of each question.

1 The volumes of the solids below have been calculated. Match each solid with its correct volume. 🔲

(U3)

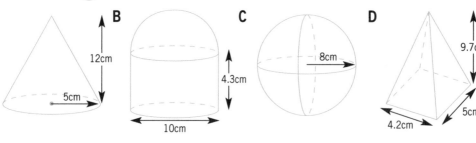

600cm³ ....   68cm³ ....   314cm³ ....   2145cm³ ....

(8 marks)

2 State whether this statement is true or false. You must
show sufficient working in order to justify your answer.

'The area of the shaded segment is 3.26cm².' 🔲

....

....

(3 marks)

Score   / 11

GCSE-style questions

Answer all parts of the questions. Show your workings (on a separate sheet of paper if necessary) and include the correct units in your answers.

1 Work out the perimeter of this sector. Give your answer to 3 significant figures. 📱

(U3)

7cm   7cm

50°

Diagram not accurately drawn

.... cm

(4 marks)

2 The sector area of a circle is 51.6cm². The radius of the circle is 9cm. Work out the size of the angle θ of the sector. Give your answer to the nearest degree. 📱

Area = 51.6cm²

9cm

θ

Diagram not accurately drawn

.... °

(3 marks)

3 The diagram shows a plastic container. The container is formed by joining a cylindrical tube to a hemisphere.

The diameter of the cylinder and hemisphere is 26cm. The total height of the container is 51cm.

Work out the volume of the container. Give your answer correct to 3 significant figures. 📱

51cm

26cm

.... m³

(4 marks)

4 The volume of a ball bearing is 268mm³. Work out the diameter of the ball bearing, giving your answer to the nearest whole number. 📱

.... mm

(3 marks)

Score   / 14

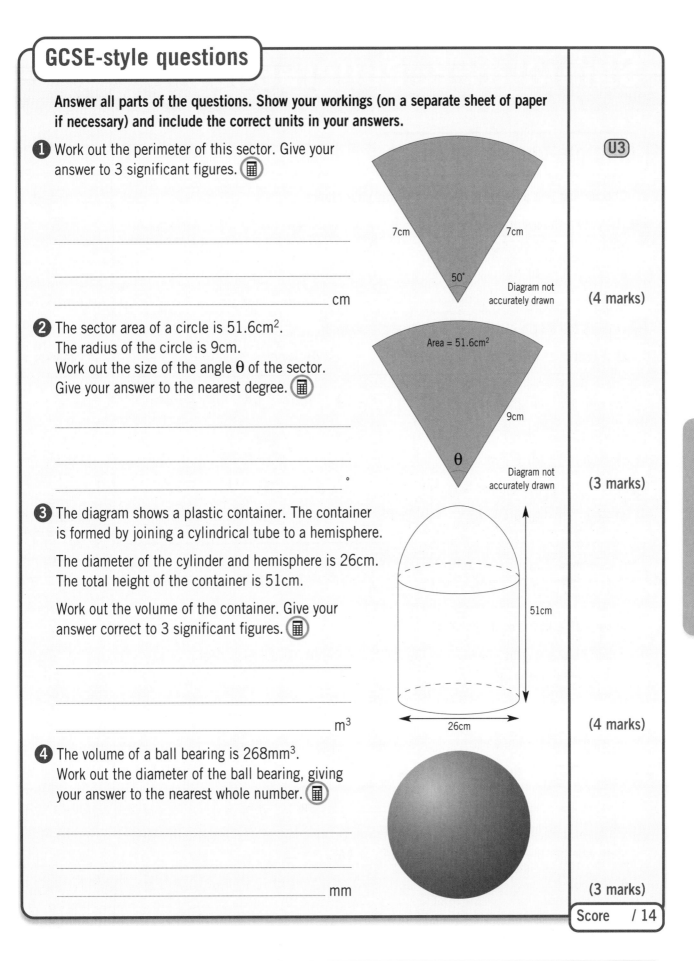

How well did you do?

| 0–8 Try again | 9–14 Getting there | 15–22 Good work | 23–30 Excellent! |

For more information on this topic, see pages 102–103 of your Success Revision Guide.

83

Similarity & congruency

Multiple-choice questions

Choose just one answer, a, b, c or d. Circle your choice.

1 These two shapes are similar. What is the size of angle *x*?

Diagrams not accurately drawn

U3

a) 90°   b) 47°

c) 53°   d) 50°

(1 mark)

2 What is the length of *y* in the larger triangle above?

a) 14cm   b) 12cm   c) 8cm   d) 16cm

(1 mark)

3 These two shapes are similar. What is the radius of the smaller cone? ▦

Diagrams not accurately drawn

a) 3cm   b) 9.6cm

c) 5cm   d) 10cm

(1 mark)

4 What is the perpendicular height of the larger cone above? ▦

a) 3cm   b) 9.16cm   c) 9cm   d) 9.26cm

(1 mark)

Score   / 4

Short-answer questions

Answer all parts of each question.

1 Calculate the lengths marked *n* in these similar shapes. Give your answers correct to 1 decimal place. ▦

U3

a)

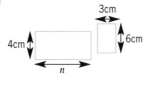

b)

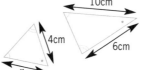

c)

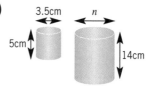

n = _____ cm   *n* = _____ cm   *n* = _____ cm

(6 marks)

2 Which of the following pairs of triangles, C and D, are congruent? For those that are, state whether the reason is SSS, RHS, SAS or AAS.

a)

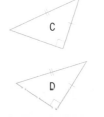

b)

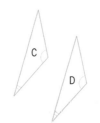

c)

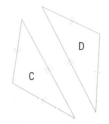

_____   _____   _____

(3 marks)

Score   / 9

GCSE-style questions

Answer all parts of the questions. Show your workings (on a separate sheet of paper if necessary) and include the correct units in your answers.

1 In the diagram, MN is parallel to YZ.
YMX and ZNX are straight lines.
XM = 4cm, XY = 14cm,
XN = 6cm, YZ = 17.5cm.

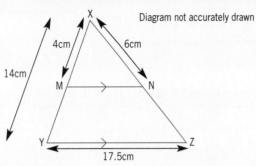

Diagram not accurately drawn

(U3)

a) Calculate the length of MN. 🖩 ....
.... cm   **(2 marks)**

b) Calculate the length of NZ. 🖩 ....
.... cm   **(2 marks)**

2 Soup is sold in two similar cylindrical cans.

a) The area of the label on the smaller can is 162cm². Calculate the area of the label on the larger can. (The labels are also similar and in the same proportion as the height of the cans.) 🖩
.... cm²   **(2 marks)**

b) The capacity of the larger can of soup is 5 litres. Calculate the capacity of the smaller can of soup. 🖩
.... litres   **(2 marks)**

3 In the diagram RS = ST = RU = TU.
Prove that the triangle RST is
congruent to triangle RUT.

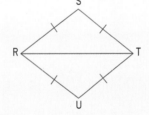

....

....   **(3 marks)**

Score   / 11

How well did you do?

| 0–7 | Try again | 8–12 | Getting there | 13–19 | Good work | 20–24 | Excellent! |

For more information on this topic, see pages 104–105 of your Success Revision Guide.

Vectors

Multiple-choice questions

Choose just one answer, a, b, c or d. Circle your choice.

1 If vector $\mathbf{a} = \binom{2}{3}$ and vector $\mathbf{b} = \binom{-5}{-2}$, what is $\mathbf{a} + \mathbf{b}$?

  a) $\binom{1}{-3}$ **b)** $\binom{-3}{1}$ **c)** $\binom{7}{-5}$ **d)** $\binom{-10}{-6}$

(U3)

(1 mark)

2 If vector $\mathbf{c} = \binom{-4}{2}$ and vector $\mathbf{d} = \binom{-6}{-5}$, what is $\mathbf{c} - \mathbf{d}$?

  a) $\binom{8}{-14}$ **b)** $\binom{-6}{-5}$ **c)** $\binom{2}{7}$ **d)** $\binom{-6}{5}$

(1 mark)

3 If vector $\mathbf{p} = \binom{7}{-2}$ and vector $\mathbf{r} = \binom{-9}{2}$, what is $4\mathbf{p} + \mathbf{r}$?

  a) $\binom{19}{-6}$ **b)** $\binom{38}{0}$ **c)** $\binom{-6}{19}$ **d)** $\binom{20}{-3}$

(1 mark)

4 Which vector is parallel to $\binom{2}{5}$?

  a) $\binom{10}{20}$ **b)** $\binom{6}{15}$ **c)** $\binom{20}{45}$ **d)** $\binom{1}{2}$

(1 mark)

5 Which vector is parallel to vector $\mathbf{r} = \binom{-4}{6}$?

  a) $\binom{-8}{6}$ **b)** $\binom{-16}{24}$ **c)** $\binom{-4}{12}$ **d)** $\binom{-8}{18}$

(1 mark)

Score   / 5

Short-answer questions

Answer all parts of each question.

1 The statements below refer to the diagram opposite. State whether the statements are true or false.

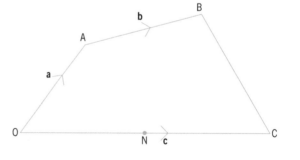

(U3)

a) $\overrightarrow{OB} = \mathbf{a} + \mathbf{b}$ (1 mark)

b) $\overrightarrow{BC} = -\mathbf{a} + \mathbf{b} + \mathbf{c}$ (1 mark)

c) $\overrightarrow{AC} = -\mathbf{a} + \mathbf{c}$ (1 mark)

d) If N is the midpoint of OC then $\overrightarrow{AN} = -\frac{1}{2}\mathbf{c} + \mathbf{a}$ (1 mark)

2 If $\overrightarrow{OC} = 2\mathbf{a} - 3\mathbf{b}$ and $\overrightarrow{OD} = 12\mathbf{a} - 18\mathbf{b}$, write down two geometrical facts about the vectors $\overrightarrow{OC}$ and $\overrightarrow{OD}$.

(2 marks)

3 On grid paper, draw the vectors **a** and **b**, then complete the statements.

  a) $\mathbf{a} = \binom{3}{2}$, $\mathbf{b} = \binom{-4}{6}$, $\mathbf{a} + \mathbf{b} = (\quad)$ **b)** $\mathbf{a} = \binom{1}{4}$, $\mathbf{b} = \binom{-2}{5}$, $\mathbf{a} - \mathbf{b} = (\quad)$

(4 marks)

Score   / 10

Answer all parts of the questions. Show your workings (on a separate sheet of paper if necessary) and include the correct units in your answers.

1 The diagram is a sketch.
A is the point (4, 3)
B is the point (6, 7)
Write down the vector $\overrightarrow{AB}$ as a column vector $\binom{x}{y}$

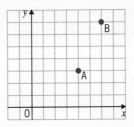

(U3)

(2 marks)

2

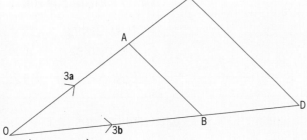

$\overrightarrow{OA} = 3\mathbf{a}$, $\overrightarrow{OB} = 3\mathbf{b}$, $\overrightarrow{OC} = 5\mathbf{a}$, $\overrightarrow{BD} = 2\mathbf{b}$
Prove that AB is parallel to CD.

(3 marks)

3

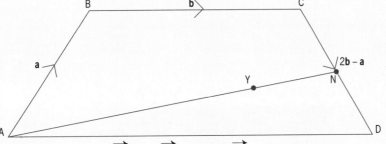

ABCD is a quadrilateral with $\overrightarrow{AB} = \mathbf{a}$, $\overrightarrow{BC} = \mathbf{b}$ and $\overrightarrow{CD} = 2\mathbf{b} - \mathbf{a}$.

a) Express $\overrightarrow{AC}$ in terms of **a** and **b**. _____ (1 mark)

b) Prove that BC is parallel to AD. _____ (2 marks)

c) N is the midpoint of CD. Express $\overrightarrow{AN}$ in terms of **a** and **b**.

(2 marks)

d) Y is the point on AN such that AY : YN = 3 : 1. Show that $\overrightarrow{YD} = \frac{3}{8}(4\mathbf{b} - \mathbf{a})$.

(3 marks)

Score   / 13

Geometry and measures

How well did you do?

| 0–6 | Try again | 7–12 | Getting there | 13–19 | Good work | 20–28 | Excellent! |

For more information on this topic, see pages 106–107 of your Success Revision Guide.

Mixed GCSE-style questions

Answer these questions. Show full working out. Use a separate sheet of paper if necessary.

1 Katy sells CDs. She sells each CD for £9.20 plus VAT at 17.5%. She sells 127 CDs. Work out how much money Katy receives.

(4 marks)

2 Here is part of Mrs Allen's electricity bill:
Work out the total cost of the electricity bill including VAT at 5%.

Electricity Bill	
New reading	11 427
Old reading	10 619
Cost per unit	12.5p

(4 marks)

3 The times, in minutes, taken to finish an assault course are listed in order.

8, 12, 12, 13, 15, 17, 22, 23, 23, 27, 29

a) i) Find the lower quartile

ii) Find the interquartile range

(2 marks)

b) Draw a box plot for this data.

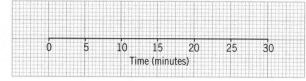

(3 marks)

4 The table gives the times to the nearest minute to complete a puzzle.

Time (minutes)	Frequency
$0 \leqslant t < 10$	5
$10 \leqslant t < 20$	12
$20 \leqslant t < 30$	8
$30 \leqslant t < 40$	5

Calculate an estimate for the mean number of minutes taken to complete the puzzle.

(4 marks)

5 Riddlington High School is holding a sponsored walk. The pupils at the school decide whether or not to take part. The probability that Afshan will take part is $\frac{2}{3}$. The probability that Bethany will take part is $\frac{4}{5}$ and the probability that Colin will take part is $\frac{1}{4}$

Calculate the probability that:

a) all three take part in the sponsored walk

(2 marks)

U1

Mixed GCSE-style questions

5 b) two of them take part in the sponsored walk

(3 marks)

6 a) Megan bought a TV for £700. Each year the TV depreciated in value by 20%.
Work out the value of the TV two years after Megan bought it.

(3 marks)

b) In a '20% off' sale, William bought a DVD player for £300.
What was the original price of the DVD player before the sale?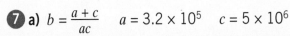

(3 marks)

7 a) $b = \dfrac{a + c}{ac}$ $a = 3.2 \times 10^5$ $c = 5 \times 10^6$

U1 | U2

Calculate the value of b. Give your answer in standard form.    (2 marks)

b) Rearrange the formula to make a the subject.   (2 marks)

8 Here are the first four terms of an arithmetic sequence:

U2

5, 9, 13, 17

Find an expression, in terms of n, for the nth term of the sequence.

(2 marks)

9 The diagram shows the position of three towns, A, B and C. Town C is due east of towns A and B. Town B is due east of A.

```
•————————————————————————•——•
A                        B  C
```

Town B is $3\frac{1}{3}$ miles from town A. Town C is $1\frac{1}{4}$ miles from town B.
Calculate the number of miles between town A and town C.

(3 marks)

10 a) Solve $5x - 2 = 3(x + 6)$ $x =$ (2 marks)

b) Solve $\dfrac{3 - 2x}{4} = 2$ $x =$ (2 marks)

c) i) Factorise $x^2 - 10x + 24$ (2 marks)

   ii) Hence, solve $x^2 - 10x + 24 = 0$ (2 marks)

d) Simplify $\dfrac{x^2 + 2x}{x^2 + 5x + 6}$ (3 marks)

e) Simplify the following:

   i) $p^4 \times p^6$ (1 mark)

   ii) $\dfrac{p^7}{p^3}$ (1 mark)

   iii) $\dfrac{p^4 \times p^5}{p}$ (1 mark)

   iv) $(p^{-\frac{1}{2}})^4$ (1 mark)

11 Prove that $0.6\overset{..}{2}\overset{..}{9}$ can be written as the fraction $\frac{623}{990}$

(2 marks)

12 a) The number 360 can be written as $2^a \times 3^b \times 5^c$.
Calculate the values of a, b and c.

(3 marks)

⑫ **b)** Find the highest common factor of 56 and 60.

.... (2 marks)

c) Find the lowest common multiple of 56 and 60.

.... (2 marks)

⑬ Prove that: $(3t + 1)^2 - (3t - 1)^2$ is a multiple of 4 for all positive values of t.

.... (3 marks)

⑭ $a = 2 + \sqrt{7}$ and $b = 2 - 3\sqrt{7}$. Simplify the following, giving your answer in the form $p + q\sqrt{7}$, where p and q are integers.

a) $a + b$ .... (3 marks)

b) a^2 .... (3 marks)

c) ab .... (3 marks)

⑮ Solve the equation $\dfrac{x - 4}{x^2 - 16} + \dfrac{2}{2x - 4} = 1$

Leave your answers in surd form. $x =$ .... (5 marks)

⑯ The diagram shows a circle of diameter 2.7m.
Work out the area of the circle. Give your answer correct to 1 decimal place.

.... m^2 (3 marks)

(U3)

⑰ The lines PQ and RS are parallel.

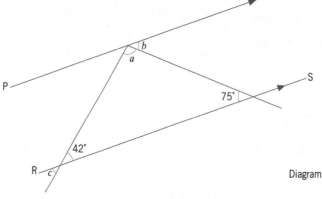

Diagram not accurately drawn

a) Write down the value of b. Give a reason for your answer.

.... (2 marks)

b) Write down the value of c. Give a reason for your answer.

.... (2 marks)

c) Write down the value of a.

.... (2 marks)

18 The diagram shows a right-angled triangle.
PQ = 14.2cm.
Angle PRQ = 90°.
Angle RPQ = 38°.

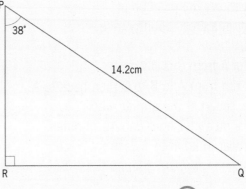

Find the length of the side QR. Give your answer to 3 significant figures.

_____ cm

(3 marks)

19

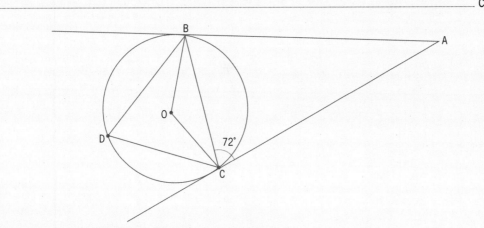

D, B and C are points on a circle with centre O.
AB and AC are tangents to the circle. Angle ACB = 72°.

a) Explain why angle OCB is 18°.

_____

(1 mark)

b) Calculate the size of angle BDC. Give reasons for your answer.

_____

_____

(3 marks)

20 The shape of a disused fish pond is a cylinder as shown. 1m³ of soil weighs 1.25 tonnes. A gardener wants to fill the pond with soil as cheaply as possible. The table shows the cost that two companies charge to do this:

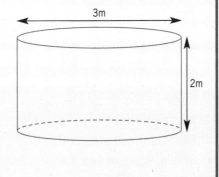

Gardener's Soil	£52 per tonne	Delivery £25
Tops' Soil	7 tonnes for £340, then £68.25 per extra tonne	Free delivery

Which company should the gardener use and how much will it cost?

_____

(6 marks)

Mixed GCSE-style questions

21 The diagram shows the position of three markers in a cross-country race.
AC is 10km.
The bearing of A from C is 302°.
The athletes run from A to B to C then back to A.
Calculate the speed of the athlete who completes the race in 1 hour and 45 minutes.
Give your answer in km/h to 1 decimal place.

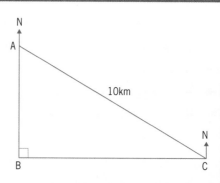

U3

(5 marks)

22 PQRS is a cyclic quadrilateral.
PS = 4.3cm, SR = 2.7cm, angle PSR = 143° and PQ = QR.

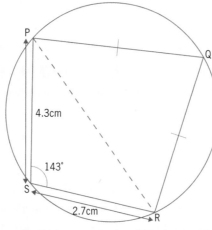

Diagram not accurately drawn

a) Calculate the length of PR. _____ cm 🖩 (3 marks)

b) Calculate the length of QR. _____ cm 🖩 (3 marks)

c) Calculate the area of triangle PQR. _____ cm² 🖩 (3 marks)

23 The diagram shows a child's toy, which is hollow. The toy is made of a cone and hemisphere. The height of the cone is 4cm. The base radius of cone and hemisphere is 3cm.

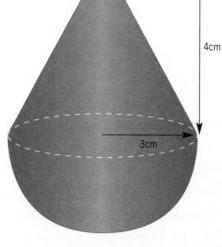

4cm

3cm

a) Work out the total surface area of the toy. Give your answer as a multiple of π.

_____ cm²

(4 marks)

b) The toy is made in two sizes. The large toy is three times the size of the toy opposite. What is the total surface area of the large toy? Give your answer as a multiple of π.

_____ cm²

Diagram not accurately drawn

(3 marks)

24 A triangular piece of metal is cut out of a rectangular piece of metal.
The length of the rectangle is $(2x + 4)$cm.
The width of the rectangle is $(x + 6)$cm.
The height of the triangle is $(x + 4)$cm.
The base of the triangle is $(x + 1)$cm.
The shaded region in the diagram shows the metal remaining.
The area of the shaded region is 38.5cm^2.

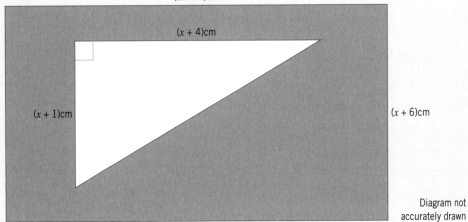

(2x + 4)cm

(x + 4)cm

(x + 1)cm

(x + 6)cm

Diagram not
accurately drawn

a) Show that $x^2 + 9x - 11 = 0$

_____

_____ (4 marks)

b) i) Solve the equation $x^2 + 9x - 11 = 0$
Give your answer correct to 3 significant figures. 🖩

_____ (3 marks)

ii) Hence find the area of the triangle.

_____ (1 mark)

25 The right-angled triangle has sides x, y and $x + 1$. x and y are integers.

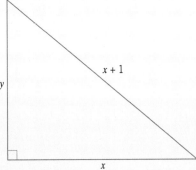

x + 1

y

x

Prove that y must be an odd number.

_____ (5 marks)

Answers to mixed questions

① $9.20 \times 1.175 = £10.81$
with VAT for each CD.
$127 \times £10.81$
$= £1372.87$

② $11\,427 - 10\,619 = 808$ units
$808 \times 12.5p = 10\,100p = £101$
VAT at 5% $= 1.05 \times 101 = £106.05$
Total bill $= £106.05$

③ a) i) lower quartile = 12

   ii) interquartile range = 11

b)
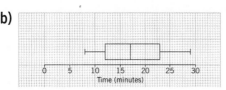

④ $19.\dot{3}$ minutes (1 d.p.)

⑤ a) $\frac{2}{15}$

   b) $\frac{1}{2}$

⑥ a) £448

   b) £375

⑦ a) 3.325×10^{-6}

   b) $a = \dfrac{c}{bc - 1}$

⑧ $4n + 1$

⑨ $4\frac{7}{12}$ miles

⑩ a) $x = 10$

   b) $x = -2.5$

   c) i) $(x - 4)(x - 6)$

      ii) $x = 4$ and $x = 6$

   d) $\dfrac{x(x + 2)}{(x + 2)(x + 3)} = \dfrac{x}{x + 3}$

   e) i) p^{10}

      ii) p^4

      iii) p^8

      iv) $p^{-2} = \dfrac{1}{p^2}$

11 Let $x = 0.629\,292\,9$
$10x = 6.292\,929$
$1000x = 629.292\,929$
$990x = 629.292\,929 - 6.292\,929$
$990x = 623$
$x = \frac{623}{990}$
Hence, $0.6\dot{2}\dot{9} = \frac{623}{990}$

12 **a)** $a = 3$, $b = 2$, $c = 1$

b) 4

c) 840

13 $(3t + 1)^2 - (3t - 1)^2$
$[(3t + 1)(3t + 1)] - [(3t - 1)(3t - 1)]$
$[(9t^2 + 6t + 1) - (9t^2 - 6t + 1)]$
$= 12t$
Since 12 is a multiple of 4, then $12t$ is a multiple of 4.

14 **a)** $4 - 2\sqrt{7}$

b) $11 + 4\sqrt{7}$

c) $-17 - 4\sqrt{7}$

15 $\frac{x-4}{x^2-16} + \frac{2}{2x-4} = 1$

$\frac{x-4}{(x-4)(x+4)} + \frac{2}{2(x-2)} = 1$

$\frac{1}{(x+4)} + \frac{1}{(x-2)} = 1$

$x - 2 + x + 4 = 1\,(x + 4)\,(x - 2)$
$2x + 2 = x^2 + 2x - 8$
$x^2 + 2x - 8 - 2x - 2 = 0$
$x^2 - 10 = 0$, $x = \pm\sqrt{10}$
$x = +\sqrt{10}$ or $x = -\sqrt{10}$

16 Area πr^2
$\pi \times 1.35^2$
$= 5.7\text{m}^2$

17 **a)** $b = 75°$ since angle b and 75° are alternate angles.

b) $c = 42°$ since angle c and 42° are vertically opposite.

c) $a = 63°$

18 14.2 sin 38 = 8.74cm

19 **a)** The radius and tangent meet at 90°.
Since angle ACB = 72° then angle OCB = 90° – 72° = 18°.

b) Angle OCB = angle OBC = 18°. Angle BOC = 180° – (2 × 18°) = 144°.
Angle BDC = 144° ÷ 2 = 72°, since the angle subtended at the centre is twice the angle at the circumference.

Answers to mixed questions

20 Volume of pond = $\pi \times r^2 \times h$
$\qquad\qquad \pi \times 1.5^2 \times 2$
$\qquad\qquad = 14.137...\text{m}^3$

Volume of soil = $\quad 14.137 \times 1.25 = 17.67$ tonnes

Gardeners' Soil $\quad 52 \times 18 + 25$
$\qquad\qquad\qquad = £961$

Tops' Soil $\qquad 340 + 11 \times 68.25$
$\qquad\qquad\qquad = £1090.75$

Gardener's Soil is the cheapest.

21 Angle ACB $= 302° - 270°$
$\qquad\qquad\quad = 32°$
Length AB $= \sin 32° \times 10$
$\qquad\qquad = 5.299...$
Length BC $= \cos 32° \times 10$
$\qquad\qquad = 8.48...$
Total distance of race $= 23.779$km
$s = d / t$
$s = 23.779 / 1.75$
Speed $= 13.6$km/h (1 d.p.)

22 a) 6.66cm (3 s.f.)

b) 10.49cm (3 s.f.)

c) 33.1cm^2 (3 s.f.)

23 a) Curved surface area of cone $= \pi r l$
$\qquad \pi \times 3 \times 5 = 15\pi\text{cm}^2$
Curved surface area of hemisphere $= \dfrac{4\pi r^2}{2}$
$2\pi \times 9 = 18\pi\text{cm}^2$
Total curved surface area $= 33\pi\text{cm}^2$

b) Linear scale factor $= 3$
Area scale factor $= 3^2 = 9$
Curved surface area of larger toy $= 9 \times 33\pi = 297\pi\text{cm}^2$

24 a) $(2x + 4)(x + 6) - \frac{1}{2} \times (x + 1)(x + 4) = 38.5$

$2x^2 + 16x + 24 - \dfrac{(x^2 + 5x + 4)}{2} = 38.5$

$4x^2 + 32x + 48 - x^2 - 5x - 4 = 77$
$3x^2 + 27x + 44 = 77$
$3x^2 + 27x - 33 = 0$
$(\div 3) \therefore x^2 + 9x - 11 = 0$

b) i) $x = 1.09$ or $x = -10.1$, but $x > 0$
ii) Area of triangle $= \frac{1}{2} \times 2.09 \times 5.09 = 5.319\,05 = 5.32\text{cm}^2$ (3 s.f.)

25 $x^2 + y^2 = (x + 1)^2$
$x^2 + y^2 = (x + 1)(x + 1)$
$x^2 + y^2 = x^2 + 2x + 1$
$y^2 = 2x + 1$
$2x$ is even so $2x + 1$ is always odd. Therefore, y^2 is odd and so y is odd when x and y are integers.